OSAGE NATION

History of Osage Indians

Beginning to Present

ADAM CLINE

Front Cover - Osage dancers

(15637, Ruth Mohler Collection, OHS)

TABLE OF CONTENTS

INTRODUCTION

In the heart of North America, where the vast expanse of the Great Plains meets the enchanting embrace of lush woodlands, lies a people that trace their roots back to the mists of ancient times. This land was inhabited by many resilient peoples, skilled hunters, and gatherers whose ancestors roamed these lands as early as 500 BCE, leaving behind whispers of their presence in the form of archaeological evidence and indigenous cultures. One of these cultures that rose to prominence was the Osage Nation.

In this book, we go on a profound journey, exploring the significant events, joys, sorrows, tragedies and miracles that have shaped this tribe's identity and spirit. With the expertise of historical scholarship and the allure of compelling storytelling, let us delve into this mesmerizing tapestry of history, where legends dance alongside facts, to gain a deeper appreciation for the Osage people's remarkable odyssey and indomitable spirit. As we uncover the layers of their history, we hope you find yourself captivated by the legacy they leave behind—a legacy that resonates not only within the Osage Nation but also in the very soul of North America itself.

Chapter One
Ancient Roots: the Beginning of the Osage Tribe

In the tapestry of time, the Osage people have left an indelible mark on history, reminding us of the extraordinary legacies that can emerge from a profound connection to the natural world. Their story beckons us to pause and contemplate the importance of respecting and cherishing our environment—a lesson that remains as relevant now as it was in the ancient past. From their origins to the apex of their civilization, it's time to unravel the threads that bound their society together and explore the pivotal moments that shaped their destiny.

Long before the first European explorers set sail to distant shores, a remarkable chapter unfolded on the North American continent— a chapter woven with the captivating tales of many indigenous tribes. Flourishing amongst these tribes was the Osage nation, a close-knit community that gracefully navigated the rhythms of nature.

The ancient migration patterns of the Osage Nation have long intrigued archaeologists, who diligently sift through the sands of time to piece together the captivating tale of their ancestors' journey and where the Osage people originated. While precise details remain shrouded in the mists of antiquity, the amalgamation of archaeological evidence and historical clues offers valuable insights into their movements and settlements.

Many centuries ago, in the prehistoric era, the Osage journey was believed to have begun in the Ohio River Valley and the Appalachian Mountains. This region, abundant with natural resources, provided a fertile ground for their development as skilled hunters and gatherers. As time flowed onward, the nation displayed its nomadic spirit, propelled by a curious yearning to explore new horizons. Why would they leave their homes? Was it war? Or simple wanderlust? The truth is that it could have been a little of both! Some assert that the Osage began migrating as early as 1200 CE.

Nomadic by nature, all of the Osage tribes followed the rhythm of the land, harmonizing their way of life with the changing seasons. Their movements were guided by the abundant resources they encountered, particularly the grand bison herds that sustained their bodies and provided materials for crafting their livelihoods. Descendants of the illustrious Mississippian culture, which flourished within the heartlands of the Ohio and Mississippi valleys, the Osage people's ancestral legacy beckoned them towards the boundless expanse of the West.

Intriguingly, the contours of Osage governance, a tapestry woven with threads of resilience and adaptation, can be traced back to the crucible of conflict with the encroaching Iroquois. The

Iroquois Wars, often referred to as the Beaver Wars, were a series of conflicts that spanned the 17th century and were primarily driven by the Iroquois Confederacy's quest for control over the fur trade, particularly the highly sought-after beaver pelts. As the Iroquois, a formidable alliance of tribes surging from the East, pursued their territorial ambitions, they displaced and disrupted many tribes in their path. Triggering a chain reaction of migrations and realignments.

While the Osage were located far to the west of the Iroquois heartland, the intense upheavals caused by these Wars created a domino effect of tribes being pushed from their ancestral lands. This displacement created migration pressure that radiated outward. As tribes closer to the eastern seaboard were displaced, they often migrated westward, encroaching on the lands inhabited by other tribes, including the Osage. It's believed the Iroquois Wars may have also disrupted trade networks and access to resources which could have affected the Osage Nation by influencing the availability of certain goods that might have previously been obtained through trade with tribes directly affected by the wars. In response, the Osage would have been motivated to explore new territories to secure now inaccessible vital resources.

The Nation's emergence stands as a turning point in their remarkable history—a period of transformation when diverse clans and groups coalesced into a unified tribe. It is a captivating story of how these tribes forged a distinct identity, setting them apart from other indigenous tribes. Their unique language, artistry, and customs intertwined to form a vibrant culture that dazzled all who encountered it. Each brushstroke of their art, each melody of their songs, and each step of their sacred dances whispered stories of a civilization in perfect harmony with its surroundings.

Over time, the Osage Nations' wanderings led them to settle in the region that would later become known as present-day Missouri and Arkansas. A wilderness rich with resources, a tapestry of colors and textures painted by Mother Nature herself The lush lands, with their harmonious blend of open prairies and wooded hills, proved to be an ideal homeland for them as a nation. Here, the Osage thrived, etching their legacy upon the very fabric of the land. Evidence of their ancient settlement in this area, include burial sites, village remnants, and artifacts that showcase their way of life. While the ancient migration patterns of the Osage Nation may not be wholly unraveled, the work of archaeologists continues to illuminate the journey of their ancestors. Through carefully analyzed artifacts, sites, and historical documents, they piece together a vivid portrait of the Osage people's migration and settlement, painting a compelling picture of a resilient and resourceful civilization that thrived amidst the ever-changing landscape of North America.

The establishment of the Osage Nation as a cohesive and thriving community can be seen in the archaeological findings of communal spaces and ceremonial sites, providing a glimpse into their shared rituals and cultural values. As the nation settled into their beloved homeland, they continued to adapt and evolve, honing their skills and knowledge of the land. Their profound understanding of the ecosystem was akin to a sacred knowledge, a divine communion that revealed the secrets of medicinal plants, the migratory patterns of animals, and the ideal locations for communal gatherings. This intricate awareness birthed a culture that not only survived but flourished for centuries—a culture deeply rooted in the rhythm of life. It is a dynamic ensemble of different tribes originating from various corners of the continent. At its core are the Osage people, also known as the "Wazhazhe," who embarked on a westward migration from the Ohio and Mississippi valleys, carving a legacy of warrior tradition and societal complexity across the Great Plains. Alongside them, the Quapaw, or "Ugákhpa," contribute their heritage rooted in the Mississippi River. At the same time, the Kansa, Ponca, and Omaha tribes infuse the Nation with their unique stories of resilience and adaptation. Together, these tribes collectively paint a vibrant picture of unity and diversity, demonstrating their remarkable resilience and vibrant tapestry.

At the heart of the Osage Nation's emergence, within its intricate social structure, the people organized themselves into clans, with each clan consisting of extended families, bound not only by blood relations but also by shared customs, traditions, and common ancestry. Clans held unique names that carried special meaning, often rooted in their ancestral heritage. They were the building blocks of the Osage social organization, and held a central and esteemed position, serving as the very backbone of their identity and kinship.

The kinship ties within the clans were a testament to the interconnectedness of Osage society. Members of a clan traced their lineage through both their maternal and paternal lines, creating a comprehensive network of familial relationships that transcended individual households. But clans were more than just family units; they were pillars of support, providing a sense of belonging and protection.This web of kinship fostered a profound sense of unity and support, ensuring that every member of the clan had a place and purpose within the larger community. In times of joy and sorrow, clan members came together to celebrate achievements or offer consolation during challenging moments. Each clan had its own specific roles and responsibilities within society. Some clans excelled in particular trades or crafts, passing down their specialized knowledge from generation to generation. Others were known for their hunting prowess, leadership, and spiritual guidance. This diversity of skills and expertise enhanced the overall strength and resilience of the Osage Nation. As the clans interacted and collaborated, they solidified the foundation of the nation's identity, shaping the tribe's values, customs, and way of life.

Interclan relationships formed a complex and dynamic web that contributed to the overall cohesion of the tribes. Intermarriages between clans further strengthened these ties, solidifying bonds and ensuring mutual support. In times of war or external threat, the clans united as a formidable force, demonstrating the strength of their collective identity. During peacetime, they worked collaboratively to secure their homeland, cultivating crops, managing resources, and ensuring the well-being of all community members. The rich tapestry of their social fabric was interwoven with kinship, tradition, and a shared sense of purpose, allowing the Nation to thrive as a close-knit community.

Within this community, at the apex of the clan structure, leaders emerged—wise and diplomatic figures who guided the tribe with foresight and tact.These respected elders possessed profound wisdom and were often skilled orators facilitating communication and unity among the clans, ensuring that decisions were made collectively and the needs of the entire tribe were considered. Their counsel was sought within the clan and in matters affecting the broader Osage nation. In cases of conflict or disagreements, the elders of the involved clans would convene to discuss and find resolutions. Their decisions were based on a deep understanding of tradition, fairness, and the greater good of the tribe.

As storytellers and custodians of oral traditions, elders held a revered place in Osage society. Weaving intricate tales of their ancestors' bravery, resilience, and wisdom. These stories passed down from generation to generation, served as a source of pride and a moral compass, imparting essential life lessons and cultural values.

Chapter Two
The Osage Way of Life

As the seasons danced and the earth's heartbeat pulsed, the Osage people synchronized their lives with nature's symphony, each season guiding their activities and ceremonies in ways that celebrated the cycles of life. In the warm embrace of spring, as the Earth awakened from its slumber, the people eagerly embraced the opportunity to plant their crops with great care. This vital time of sowing and nurturing symbolized renewal and hope, and it was a testament to their deep respect for the fertile soil that sustained them. With each seed carefully placed in the earth. The Osage people invoked prayers for a bountiful harvest, acknowledging the sacred bond they shared with the land.

Successful agricultural knowledge and techniques were cultivated through generations, fostering a sense of continuity and shared wisdom. Rooted in a profound respect for the land and a sustainable set of beliefs, their cultivation practices were a testament to their astute understanding of nature's rhythms and ability to adapt and thrive in a sometimes unforgiving environment. Central to their approach was the concept of sustainable agriculture, a notion that guided their actions in cultivating the land. Through the strategic practice of crop rotation, the Osage ensured that the soil remained nutrient-rich and avoided the depletion that often plagues monoculture farming. This mindful practice allowed them to maintain the fertility of their fields over time, sustaining their food production and reducing the risk of crop failures. Among the most remarkable techniques they employed was the renowned "Three Sisters" intercropping method. This ingenious strategy involved planting corn, beans, and squash together in the same plot. The corn provided a sturdy structure for the beans to climb, while the beans enriched the soil with nitrogen—a nutrient crucial for plant growth. Meanwhile, the sprawling squash plants acted as natural ground cover, suppressing weed growth and conserving soil moisture. This intricate dance of vegetation showcased the Osage's holistic understanding of ecological relationships, resulting in a synergy that optimized yields while minimizing resource use.

In response to the semi-arid nature of the Great Plains, the Osage ingeniously utilized terracing and water management techniques as well. By constructing terraces into the hillsides, they effectively controlled erosion and captured rainwater, allowing it to seep into the soil and nourish their crops gradually. This innovative method not only conserved precious water resources but also protected against the unpredictable nature of droughts, which could devastate unprepared crops. The Osage's seed selection practices reflected their intimate knowledge of their environment. Through generations of observation and experimentation, they identified seeds with attributes like drought resistance and disease tolerance, ultimately yielding crops well-suited to their ecosystem. Additionally, controlled burning emerged as a powerful land management tool. By deliberately setting fires at specific times, the Osage effectively cleared away dead vegetation, invigorating the land and promoting the growth of edible plants, especially those with nutritional or medicinal value.

In parallel to their agricultural endeavors, hunting played a central role in Osage life. The vast expanses of the Great Plains were home to various wildlife, with the buffalo occupying a central place in their subsistence strategies. Buffaloes provided meat, hides for clothing and shelter, bones for tools, and sinews for binding. The Osage also hunted deer, utilizing their hides and antlers, while small game like rabbits and squirrels added to their protein intake. Fishing is another vital practice, leveraging the proximity to rivers and water bodies to gather aquatic resources. This hunting and gathering approach was complemented by the Osage's knowledge of edible plants, as they collected berries, nuts, and other wild foods. Their diet emerged as a harmonious fusion of cultivated crops, carefully chosen based on their mutual benefits and the diverse resources the Great Plains landscape offered.

Spring also brought forth a season of spiritual ceremonies that celebrated the reawakening of nature. They gathered in sacred spaces to express their gratitude for the bountiful gifts provided by the Earth and to seek the guidance and blessings of the spirits. These ceremonies were filled with song, dance, and offerings to honor the interconnectedness of all living beings. Spiritual ceremonies held great significance within Osage society. They were moments of reverence and communion with the spiritual realm as the entire community sought guidance, protection, and blessings. The collective participation in these ceremonies fostered a deep sense of interconnectedness with the land, their ancestors, and the divine forces that governed their lives. The communal nature of these ceremonies also provided emotional and psychological support to individuals and families during challenging times. In moments of loss or adversity, the community came together to offer solace, reinforcing the Osage belief in the strength and resilience of their shared bonds.

Spirituality permeated every facet of Osage life, with shamans and spiritual leaders serving as bridges between the human and spiritual realms. Their guidance and healing practices brought balance and well-being to individuals and the community, fostering a sense of collective spiritual harmony. The Osage people's collective spirit was further fortified through ceremonies that marked both joyous occasions and solemn moments. Rooted in symbolism and spirituality, these rituals strengthened their bond as a tribe, honoring their ancestors, seeking guidance from the spiritual realm, and expressing their deep connection to the land they called home.

In the heart of the Osage Nation, the rhythm of daily life revolved around the pursuit of sustenance and the preservation of their rich cultural heritage. The people embraced a seamless interplay of practicality and spirituality daily, paying homage to the natural world that sustained them. One of their most important sources of sustenance included the mighty bison herds that inhabited the great plains. As skilled hunters, they embarked on hunts with a deep sense of reverence and appreciation, as the bison held great importance as a source of food, clothing, and materials for their everyday needs. Before setting out on such a momentous endeavor, the tribe engaged in solemn ceremonies, seeking the blessing of the spirits and showing respect for the life they were about to take.

During bison hunts, experienced and skilled hunters were chosen to lead the endeavor. These hunters were adept at tracking and taking down their prey and well-versed in the spiritual rituals accompanying the hunt. Their knowledge of the bison's behavior, migration patterns, and the terrain they roamed was essential in ensuring the hunt's success and the tribe's survival. Armed with bows and arrows, the hunters approached their quarry with great care and precision. Their finely crafted bows, made from durable materials such as wood and sinew, were complemented by arrows adorned with skillfully crafted stone or metal points. These weapons, honed through generations of craftsmanship, allowed the Osage hunters to strike their prey accurately and efficiently. Once a successful hunt had taken place, the Osage people's communal bonds came into play again. The entire tribe would come together to process the bison, wasting nothing of the precious animal. Every part of the bison was utilized, from its meat and hide to its bones and sinew, each serving a specific purpose within their daily lives.

As the heat of summer enveloped the land, the Osage people turned their attention to nurturing their crops with great dedication. Their toil in the fields was a testament to their commitment to ensuring a successful harvest. During these warm months, the tribe sought moments of respite in ceremonies that honored the spirits of the land and sought their blessings for a fruitful harvest. One of which being the "Big Moon" ceremony, which held a special place at the heart of the Osage annual calendar. The "Big Moon Ceremony" is a sacred and significant event deeply rooted in the cultural tapestry of the Nation. It is a time of renewal, reflection, and communal unity, where tradition and spirituality intertwine to create a profoundly meaningful experience. Taking place during the month of June, the "Big Moon Ceremony" coincides with the emergence of the full moon, which holds spiritual significance for the Osage people. The ceremony typically spans several days, during which the community comes together to engage in a series of rituals, dances, and prayers. The location of the ceremony is carefully chosen, often within a natural setting that aligns with the Osage people's deep reverence for the land.

Central to the ceremony are the dances, each carrying its unique symbolism. One of the most notable dances is the "Inlonshka," also known as the "Rain Dance." This dance is performed to seek blessings from the spirits for bountiful crops, ensuring the sustenance of the community. Dancers adorned in intricate regalia move in rhythmic patterns, their steps mirroring the intertwined nature of the environment and humanity. Sharing stories, myths, and cultural teachings is another essential component of the "Big Moon" Ceremony. Elders pass down wisdom to the younger generations, ensuring the continuity of knowledge. These stories connect to the past, reinforcing the Nation's identity and values. Throughout the ceremony, offerings are made to the spirits, expressing gratitude for the land's resources and seeking their continued guidance and protection. The Osage believe that their ancestors are present during the ceremony, and their participation is acknowledged through rituals that honor their memory and contributions to the community. The "Big Moon Ceremony" isn't merely an event but a profound spiritual experience encompassing the people's cosmology, traditions, and collective consciousness. It reaffirms their bond with the land, respect for all living beings, and commitment to maintaining harmony within the natural world. As the moon's glow illuminates the ceremonial grounds, the Osage people stand united, weaving their past, present, and future into a vibrant tapestry of culture and spirituality.

With the arrival of autumn, the Osage were rewarded for their diligent work as the fruits of their labor bore witness to their skillful cultivation. During this time of harvest, families worked hand in hand, tending to their crops and gardens with shared enthusiasm and diligence. This communal approach to agriculture ensured that no individual family was left to bear the burden alone, and the fruits of their labor were distributed among the entire community. The harvest season was a time of jubilation and thanksgiving as the entire tribe gathered to celebrate the abundance provided by nature and the collective efforts that sustained them throughout the year. They expressed their gratitude in prayer and through communal feasts, sharing the fruits of their labor with one another. These meals were not mere acts of sustenance but meaningful occasions for coming together, strengthening bonds, and reaffirming their sense of unity. With gratitude and respect, they partook in the nourishment provided by the land, the animals, and their shared efforts.

As the sun set, gatherings around crackling fires were the perfect backdrop for storytelling sessions. The elders, revered for their wisdom, skillfully recounted tales of their ancestors' bravery, resilience, and wisdom. These stories were more than entertainment; they served as a moral compass, imparting cultural values and life lessons to the younger generations, The daily life of the Osage Nation was a harmonious dance, a delicate interplay between the tangible and the spiritual, underpinned by a profound connection with nature and a steadfast commitment to their communal bonds. Through their skilled hunts, shared meals, and the timeless tales shared around the fire, the Osage nurtured a way of life that celebrated their rich cultural heritage, fostered unity, and ensured their survival in the ever-changing landscape of North America.

As winter's chill descended upon the land, the Nation settled into a time of reflection and preparation. The long evenings around the warmth of hearths were dedicated to preserving their rich oral traditions and the wisdom of their ancestors. Spiritual ceremonies during the winter months held deep significance, providing solace and hope as the tribe sought guidance and protection for the tribe during the challenging times ahead. As the seasons unfolded and the years passed, the Osage Nation flourished, and with them their artistic and creative endeavors. Art and craftsmanship thrived, with intricate beadwork, distinctive pottery, and woven textiles, a vivid testament to the depth of their cultural heritage and the integral role that artistic expression plays in their lives. With a rich legacy that spans generations, these creative endeavors are imbued with profound meanings, reflecting their spiritual beliefs, historical narratives, and the strong bond they share with their ancestral lands.

One of their most renowned art forms is beadwork, characterized by intricate designs that adorn clothing, accessories, and ceremonial regalia. This meticulous craft isn't solely about aesthetics; it weaves intricate stories, depicting cultural symbols and historical events. Each bead stitched onto clothing or other items carries layers of significance, connecting the wearer with their heritage and the wider community. Another noteworthy aspect of their artistry is pottery. Its distinctive forms and intricate designs, often incorporating geometric patterns and natural motifs mark Osage pottery. These vessels serve both utilitarian and symbolic purposes. They hold the stories of generations, depicting the tribe's connections to the earth and their understanding of the delicate balance between humanity and nature.

The cultural significance of Osage arts and crafts is profound. These creative expressions serve as a bridge that spans time, connecting the modern generations with their roots and allowing them to celebrate their identity. They're not merely decorations or artifacts; they encapsulate the essence of Osage life and transmit the teachings of their elders to new generations. Inspired by the natural world around them, these creations expressed their deep connection to their environment and the stories woven into the fabric of their culture. Furthermore, Osage art often expresses itself in dance, music, and storytelling. Traditional dances, accompanied by rhythmic drumming and singing, unite the community, reinforcing their cultural bonds and invoking spiritual connections with their ancestors. Storytelling, an age-old tradition, carries narratives that teach lessons, preserve historical events, and share the wisdom accumulated over time.

Another essential part of the Osage Nations culture is the language. Belonging to the Dhegihan family of the Siouan language, served as the linguistic thread that bound the tribe together. The Osage language carries the echoes of generations past, its phonetic nuances, distinct syntax, and vocabulary are vessels that transmit not only practical communication but also the intangible essence of Osage's identity. This language serves as a bridge that spans time, connecting contemporary Osage individuals with their roots and allowing them to access the wisdom of their elders. Central to the language is its unique polysynthetic nature, where complex words are constructed by combining various elements to convey intricate meanings. This structure allows speakers to express nuanced concepts concisely, fostering a profound understanding of the world around them. Through this linguistic lens, the Osage people encode their perceptions of nature, relationships, and cultural values, preserving their heritage within the very fabric of their speech. Language becomes a living testament resonating with the echoes of generations past and the promise of generations to come.

The Osages' nurtured cultural and communal bonds facilitated the efficient sharing of knowledge, skills, and resources. Expertise in various crafts, trades, and agricultural practices was disseminated throughout the community, ensuring the optimal use of available resources and the ability to adapt to changing circumstances. The survival of the Osage tribe was intricately tied to their unwavering commitment to communal bonds, which through collaboration, mutual support, and shared cultural practices, allowed them to weather the challenges of time and history.

As neighboring tribes observed the flourishing Osage Nation, alliances and trade relationships naturally formed. These interactions enriched Osage culture, introducing new customs, materials, and ideas that were skillfully integrated into their way of life. The Osage were not insular but embraced the opportunities for cultural exchange, which only strengthened their vibrant tapestry of traditions—the 17th century brought European explorers to American shores. Faced with these encounters, the Nation approached them with both curiosity and caution. Trade with the European arrivals introduced the Osage to new goods and tools that expanded their horizons and enhanced their daily lives even more. However, these interactions also presented challenges, as the changing geopolitical landscape brought external pressures to bear upon the people's sovereignty and way of life.

Despite these external pressures, the communal bonds within the Osage nation acted as a power safeguard against threats and challenges. The strength derived from their unity meant the Osage stood united in times of conflict, forming a formidable force to protect their homeland and way of life.. They skillfully negotiated with European powers, balancing diplomacy with the imperative to protect their lands and resources. These diplomatic efforts allowed the Osage Nation to preserve a degree of autonomy during a time when indigenous sovereignty was increasingly threatened. Their shared customs, language, and vision for the future bound them tightly together like the fabric of a vibrant tapestry.

CHAPTER THREE
EUROPEAN ENCOUNTERS AND COLONIAL INFLUENCE

As the sun dipped below the horizon, casting hues of orange and purple across the vast prairies, a new chapter in Osage history began—a chapter shaped by the dramatic encounters with European explorers and the unfolding influence of colonial powers. As we step back into the annals of history, we find ourselves immersed in the breathtaking landscapes of the North American prairies, and the late 17th century as intrepid European explorers brought the winds of change, setting forth on their quest for new lands and untapped resources. As they gazed upon the uncharted territories, little did they know that their interactions with this land's indigenous communities would shape a compelling and transformative chapter in Osage (and world) history.

In the vast wilderness of the New World, two bold French adventurers,Jacques Marquette and Canadian born, Louis Jolliet, embarked on a daring expedition down the mighty Mississippi River in 1673. As their canoes glided through the river's majestic waters, they were blissfully unaware of the momentous meeting that awaited them downstream. It was a meeting that held tremendous significance for both parties involved. For the Osage people, who had thrived in their pristine and untouched landscape, the arrival of these strangers from across the sea sparked a mix of curiosity and uncertainty. The Europeans, clad in garments completely foreign to the Osage and wielding tools with designs they had never seen before, seemed like envoys from a distant realm. The encounter with these explorers must have been akin to a meeting with inhabitants from another world entirely. As Louis Jolliet and Jacques Marquette laid their eyes upon the vast prairies, dense woodlands, and the unique customs and wisdom of the Osage, they found themselves utterly captivated by the richness and beauty of this unfamiliar land. With their deep connection to nature and flourishing communities, they presented a striking contrast to the world they had left behind in Europe.

While language proved to be a barrier, gestures of goodwill and curiosity bridged the cultural divide between the two groups. An atmosphere of camaraderie and mutual interest emerged through simple exchanges of small trinkets and goods. The explorers' openness and amicability, along with the Osage people's inquisitive nature, laid the very foundations for future encounters and trade relationships that would shape the course of Osage-European relations. Jolliet and Marquette returned from this encounter with a sense of awe and wonder, deeply impressed by the untamed beauty of the American frontier and the wisdom of its native inhabitants. Their journals and accounts conveyed the enchantment they experienced during this meeting with a different culture. These journals serve as invaluable historical documents, offering intricate insights into their remarkable journey through uncharted territories of North America during the late 17th century. As Marquette and Joliet traversed the waterways of the Mississippi River and its tributaries, their detailed observations and interactions with indigenous peoples unveiled a wealth of knowledge about the land's geography, flora, fauna, and the cultures they encountered.

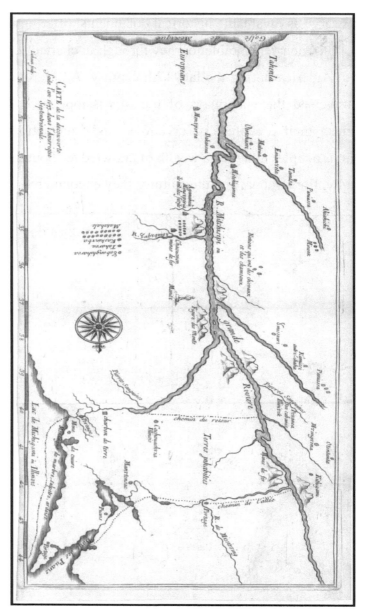

Marquette and Jolliet's journey was the first to determine the courses of rivers running through the interior of the North American continent, as illustrated in a 1681 map based on their expedition by Melchisedech Thevenot. (Library of Congress)

In their journals, Marquette and Joliet meticulously recorded their encounters with various Native American tribes, detailing their customs, languages, and ways of life. These descriptions gave European audiences a window into the indigenous world and laid the foundation for later explorations and interactions. The explorers' journals were a bridge between two vastly different worlds, sparking curiosity and fascination among their European contemporaries. Communication with their respective countries about their discoveries was critical to Marquette and Joliet's expedition. Their journals, filled with vivid descriptions and detailed maps, formed the basis of their reports to their sponsors and the authorities back home. These written accounts were vital in conveying the potential of the newly explored territories for trade, colonization, and expansion.

Back in their home countries, the information in Marquette and Joliet's journals ignited widespread interest and curiosity. Their insights into the river systems and the vast expanse of North America captured the imagination of European audiences and fueled further explorations. Their journals provided a tangible glimpse into the unknown, inspiring subsequent generations of explorers and adventurers to seek out new horizons. As they continued their voyage and explored further into the heart of the New World, the memory of their meeting with the Osage remained etched in their minds. Their writings would go on to contribute to the growing body of knowledge about the diverse indigenous peoples they encountered during their expedition.

The meeting of Louis Jolliet and Jacques Marquette with the Osage people marked the beginning of a complex and multifaceted relationship between these two distinct worlds. Through their mutual curiosity and willingness to engage with one another, they set in motion a chain of events that would have lasting consequences on not only the Osage Nation but European exploration in the New World as a whole. As explorers from various European powers continued their ventures into the heartland of America, they encountered the Osage and delved even deeper into their lives and communities.

Marquette and Jolliet traveled 2,000 miles from upper Michigan to Arkansas, including a portage near what is now Chicago. (Encyclopedia Britannica)

Among the later French explorers who encountered the Osage were renowned individuals like Robert de La Salle and esteemed fur trader Henry de Tonty. These explorers, like Louis Jolliet and Jacques Marquette before them, found themselves captivated by the vast prairies, dense woodlands, and the rich culture of the Osage people. Robert de La Salle, a visionary explorer driven by the desire to establish French territorial claims in North America, embarked on expeditions that involved navigating the Mississippi River and engaging with various indigenous nations. La Salle's curiosity and eagerness to build diplomatic relationships led to meetings with the Osage. Tonty, renowned for his resourcefulness and loyalty, joined La Salle on exploratory missions, fostering diplomatic ties with them and other indigenous groups they encountered. Their encounters with the Osage were characterized by respect and diplomacy, laying the groundwork for potential trade and cooperation.

As the exchange of goods and resources expanded, both cultures reaped the benefits of this newfound connection. The Osage, known for their curiosity and openness to the world, eagerly embraced European technologies and materials. The introduction of European goods brought about profound changes, with far reaching impacts on their material culture and daily lives, from new tools and weaponry to textiles and other commodities. These items facilitated more efficient tasks and enhanced their textile and clothing traditions.

On the other side of this cultural equation, the Europeans were equally enthralled by the abundance of the American frontier. The vast lands and untamed wilderness they encountered were a source of awe and wonder as they realized the untapped potential for exploration and trade in these uncharted territories. The ensuing encounters with the Osage people left an indelible impression on the European explorers. They admired the Osage's intimate knowledge of the land and their harmonious way of life with nature. Their deep spiritual connection to their surroundings, intricate social structures, and rich traditions left a lasting impact on the European explorers, challenging their own perceptions of the world.

These meetings set in motion a continuous stream of interactions that would shape the course of history for both the Osage Nation and the Europeans. As trade networks expanded and diplomatic ties were forged, the cultural exchange between the two worlds became increasingly intricate and interwoven. Trade enriched both cultures, introducing the Osage to novel technologies and materials that expanded their horizons while the European traders discovered new markets to explore in this uncharted land. With the passage of time, these trade networks burgeoned, becoming vital conduits for the flow of knowledge and ideas. Guided by their unyielding curiosity, the Osage gained valuable insights into European customs and practices. Their interactions with the European traders were akin to a fascinating cultural exchange program as they marveled at the Osage way of life and the abundance of the American frontier. A beautiful tapestry of cross-cultural understanding unfolded through these exchanges, transcending language barriers and nurturing amicable relations between two distinct worlds.

Amidst these intriguing exchanges, the Osage people faced challenges and uncertainties, too. As trade benefits unfurled like petals, so did the thorns of unforeseen challenges. While fascinating and enriching, the introduction of European goods and technologies to the Osage landscape also disrupted their traditional economic systems, fundamentally altering their trade networks, resource utilization, and social dynamics. European goods, such as metal tools, firearms, cloth, and beads, quickly became valuable commodities that the Osage could exchange for furs, food, and other resources. This influx of European items reshaped their trade relationships, expanding their interactions beyond neighboring tribes to include European settlers and traders.

While European goods opened up avenues for economic advancement, they also introduced specific challenges. Dependency on European items gradually shifted the Osage away from their traditional crafting and production methods. This transformation had repercussions for indigenous skills and crafts, leading to a decline in the production of traditional items like beadwork and pottery.

Furthermore, the availability of European goods led to economic disparities within the clans. Those who controlled access to European items could accumulate wealth and influence, leading to shifts in power dynamics within the community. This change in economic hierarchy sometimes led to social tensions and reshaped the Osage society's internal structure. As the dynamics of resource distribution shifted within their communities, the Osage faced the daunting task of adapting to these changes without compromising their cherished communal way of life. This delicate balance between embracing novelty and preserving tradition became a formidable challenge for the Osage people.

As European settlements began to grow the region's geopolitical dynamics underwent a profound shift. The Osage Nation found itself walking a precarious tightrope between adaptation to the encroaching colonial presence and the steadfast preservation of their ancestral lands and autonomy. Treaty-making became a pivotal mechanism for engaging with the colonial powers, but the negotiations were often intricate and uneven. Though sometimes instrumental in maintaining peace, these agreements also led to significant territorial losses for the Osage Nation. Communal land ownership, which had been a cornerstone of their culture, faced unprecedented pressures under these changing political circumstances.

In tandem with territorial concerns, the encroachment of European influence also left an indelible mark on the Osages culture and social fabric. European practices and customs found their way into the heart of Osage society, which they met with remarkable resilience and diplomatic acumen amid this delicate dance between tradition and change. Realizing the shifting power dynamics, they sought strategic alliances with European powers, skillfully navigating the intricate geopolitical landscape to protect their interests and maintain a measure of autonomy. Their efforts to forge fruitful relationships with these colonial forces showcased a keen awareness of the importance of adaptability in safeguarding their unique way of life. As we venture deeper into the enthralling Osage history, we shall witness how the echoes of these early encounters and the subsequent colonial influences reverberated through generations, shaping the destiny of the Nation.

CHAPTER FOUR
IMPACT OF TRADE, DISEASE, AND COLONIZATION

In the grand theater of history, an unseen and devastating villain emerged—infectious diseases from the Old World. The introduction of new diseases, to which the Native Americans had no immunity, had a profound and tragic impact. European diseases such as smallpox, measles, influenza, and others rapidly spread through indigenous communities, decimating populations lacking the antibodies to fight these illnesses. The Osage, who had developed their own unique way of life in the heart of the North American continent, faced a dire challenge as these diseases tore through their ranks. The toll was staggering, resulting in loss of life on an unprecedented scale. Their close-knit communities were shattered by illness, leading to the loss of elders, storytellers, and traditional knowledge-keepers. The devastating impact on their population disrupted their social fabric, strained their ability to maintain their land and resources, and forever altered the balance of power within their society.

The spread of diseases also had implications for the Osage Nation's relationship with neighboring tribes and European settlers. The weakened state of indigenous communities made them susceptible to exploitation, displacement, and the erosion of their traditional territories. European powers often took advantage of the chaos caused by their diseases to exert greater control over indigenous lands and resources. The loss of life, disruption of social structures, and erosion of cultural heritage shook the very foundations of the Nation. Traditional family systems were shattered and their once-thriving villages were now haunted by loss and grief.

As the tides of history surged forward, so did the shadows of colonization. The Osage Nation experienced a profound and intricate transformation due to colonization's impact.. The territorial consequences were significant as European expansion led to their displacement from their ancestral lands. Alongside this, the infiltration of European cultural influences threatened their identity, eroding indigenous traditions, languages, and spiritual practices. This period also witnessed political realignments, driven by European manipulation of internal tribal dynamics, which at times led to shifts in Osage leadership and power struggles.

Despite these challenges, the Osage recognized the importance of forging alliances with European powers and neighboring tribes to safeguard their interests and territorial integrity. They engaged in astute negotiations and maintained a delicate balance between accommodating external influences and preserving their cultural identity. However, the pursuit of sovereignty and autonomy was not without its challenges. The unequal power dynamics in treaty negotiations often tilted in favor of the settlers, leading to the loss of significant portions of the Osage's ancestral territory. One notable event that underscored the complexities of these negotiations was the Treaty of Paris in 1763. The treaty marked the end of the French and Indian War and resulted in the cession of French territories to Great Britain.

The victorious British Empire emerged as the dominant colonial power. Consequently, the Osage people faced a new foreign power with its own ambitions in the region. Under the terms of the Treaty of Paris, France ceded vast territories in North America to Great Britain, including parts of the Mississippi River Valley, which encompassed Osage lands. The impact of the Treaty of Paris on the Osage Nation cannot be overstated. It marked a turning point in their interactions with European powers as they transitioned from dealing primarily with French explorers to navigating the ambitions and policies of the British Empire. With the arrival of British settlers and administrators in the newly acquired territories, the Osage leaders observed the encroachment of British interests, and recognized the need for strategic diplomacy to protect their ancestral lands and traditions. Engaging in diplomatic efforts, they sought to negotiate treaties and alliances that would safeguard their territorial boundaries and assert their sovereignty. In the 18th century, they skillfully navigated relationships with French, Spanish, and American authorities, leveraging their knowledge of trade dynamics and forging alliances that allowed them to assert a degree of control over their affairs.

The British however, sought to expand their influence and control over the indigenous populations, which led to the issuance of the Royal Proclamation of 1763. This proclamation responded to the Pontiac's Rebellion, an uprising of several Native American tribes against British expansion in the Ohio River Valley. The Royal Proclamation sought to establish a boundary line between the British colonies and Native American territories, including the lands of the Osage. The intention was to prevent further conflict and regulate settlement in the region. The Royal Proclamation of 1763 recognized the importance of indigenous land rights and established a policy of negotiating treaties with Native tribes to acquire land. While this proclamation provided some measure of recognition for the sovereignty of Native American nations, it also became a point of contention between the British and the Osage.

The following century saw the Osage Nation continue to engage in treaty negotiations with the British and the newly independent United States after the American Revolution. In the early 19th century, as the United States expanded westward, the Osage entered into treaties aiming to delineate their territorial boundaries and ensure their sovereignty. The 1808 Osage-U.S. treaty exemplifies this, where the Osage secured recognition of their lands and rights while acknowledging U.S. jurisdiction.However this same treaty also resulted in the cession of a substantial portion of their ancestral lands in the regions now comprising Missouri and Arkansas..

As the United States solidified its identity as a new nation, the Osage people confronted even more challenges that tested the very fabric of their autonomy. The young nation's westward expansion brought about a series of policies including the infamous "Indian Removal" policy, which gained traction in the early 19th century. Nevertheless the Osage Nation persevered through strategic alliances and deft negotiations, seeking to safeguard their cherished way of life amidst the ever-encroaching waves of settlers. Pursuing self-governance and the quest for autonomy became a beacon of hope, guiding them through these turbulent times. Standing as a testament to the resilience of the Osage people, who weathered the storms of colonization, the devastation of disease, and the ever-changing tides of history, leaving behind a legacy that continues to resonate through the ages.

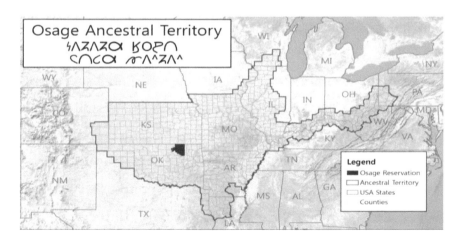

CHAPTER FIVE
A TRAIL OF TEARS

In the ever-unfolding tapestry of history, the 19th century marked a dark and turbulent chapter for native nations, the Osage included. As the United States expanded its boundaries westward, the policy of "Indian Removal" cast a shadow of uncertainty over indigenous communities. This was a moment of reckoning for the Osage —the forced relocation policy threatened to uproot them from the very land that held sacred memories and deep spiritual significance. It was not merely a matter of leaving behind physical territories; it meant severing a connection to their heritage that ran through the very soil beneath their feet.

In the face of the immense adversity brought by the Indian Removal policy, the Osage people demonstrated a spirit of incredible resilience. Gathering their strength, they embarked on a remarkable journey of negotiations with the U.S. government, unwaveringly determined to safeguard their territorial sovereignty and preserve the deep-rooted connections to their ancestral lands. In 1825, the Osage Nation signed the first of several crucial treaties. The treaty of 1825, or the First Treaty of Prairie du Chien, was an essential diplomatic effort by the Osage to protect their interests and secure their future amidst the rapidly shifting political landscape. In this treaty, the Osage reluctantly agreed to cede substantial portions of their ancestral lands to the United States.

As part of the treaty's terms, the Nation received promises from the U.S. government of new territories in the west, where they could establish their new homelands. These assurances held the hope of continuity and the preservation of their way of life in the face of the wrenching upheaval. However, as history often tells us, these promises would turn out to be hollow and unfulfilled. The assurances given to the Osage people in the treaty of 1825 soon crumbled under the weight of broken promises and unmet expectations. The lands promised in the west were not as fertile or bountiful as they had hoped. Moreover, the new territories were not immune to further pressures from westward expansion and encroachment by outsiders seeking to exploit the region's resources.

Yet, despite the mounting challenges and disappointments, they stood firm in their determination to persevere. They sought to protect their culture, traditions, and the spiritual significance of their ancestral lands. Throughout the 19th century, they navigated the complexities of coexisting with external influences while fiercely safeguarding their heritage. The treaty of 1825 was just the beginning of a series of negotiations that the Osage Nation would engage in with the U.S. government. Subsequent treaties would further redefine their lands and territories and political and economic standing.

However, perhaps one of the darkest chapters in Osage history was written with the passage of the Indian Removal Act in 1830. Meant to primarily target the Cherokee, this act authorized the government to negotiate treaties with Native American tribes, exchanging their ancestral lands in the southeastern United States for new lands west of the Mississippi River. Passed by Congress and signed into law by President Andrew Jackson, the "Indian Removal Act" required the government to negotiate removal treaties fairly, voluntarily and peacefully. It did not permit the president nor anyone else to coerce Native nations into giving up their ancestral lands. The letter of the Law however, was frequently ignored and under the iron fist of President Andrew Jackson, many indigenous communities were forced to leave their ancestral lands and endure the treacherous journey into what became known as "Indian Territory".

In 1835, the U.S. government pressured the Osage into signing a treaty, which led to the cession of a vast portion of their territory in present-day Arkansas and Missouri. This loss of land dealt a significant blow and as a result, the Osage, like many other Native American tribes, were forcibly relocated to lands in present-day Oklahoma. Entire nations were uprooted, communities were torn apart, families forced from their homes, and a rich cultural heritage was left behind. Becoming known as the "trail of tears", the forced march to "Indian Territory" was marked by hardships such as exposure to harsh weather, lack of adequate provisions, and the spread of disease. Like many others who experienced the trail of tears the Osage became victim to a staggering loss of life, immense suffering, immeasurable loss, and the rupture of their social fabric.

Amidst this heart-wrenching upheaval, the Osage people clung steadfastly to their cultural identity. They recognized that their heritage was an unbreakable thread, woven intricately into the fabric of their being, binding them to their past and guiding them into the future. The preservation of their language, traditions, and customs became an act of resilience—a powerful declaration that the essence of who they were would endure even in the face of adversity.

Whilst the relocation impacted the Osage individually it also brought them into contact with other indigenous communities sharing similar trials. One of these notable encounters was with the Cherokee Nation, another tribe subjected to the same harsh realities of the Indian Removal Act. The Osage and Cherokee found common ground in their shared struggles, and their interactions led to the exchange of stories, knowledge about survival in new lands, and the sharing of strategies to maintain cultural practices amidst adversity. Among their many interactions, the Osage also engaged with the Muscogee(Creek) Nation. The Muscogee people, experienced in navigating the shifting dynamics of colonial and indigenous interactions, provided insights into the challenges of adapting to changing circumstances while holding onto traditional values. This interaction proved to be a valuable source of wisdom for the Osage as they grappled with their own journey of adaptation.

The Osage's encounter with the Choctaw Nation revealed the power of cultural solidarity. The Choctaw, having experienced their own forced removal earlier, extended a hand of empathy to the Osage. Sharing stories and survival strategies became a means of emotional support, reminding both nations that they were not alone in their struggles. The Osage Nation's commitment to preserving their language, history, and traditions remained unwavering amid these interactions. The exchange of cultural practices with other tribes enriched their own understanding of identity and resilience. The Osage's complex linguistic heritage found commonalities and distinctions in the languages of the tribes they encountered, leading to a broader appreciation of indigenous languages' significance in preserving heritage. While shared hardships often marked the interactions, they also presented opportunities for the Osage Nation to reflect on their unique cultural attributes. These encounters underscored the importance of both adapting to change and remaining steadfast in preserving one's distinctive identity. The Osage learned through dialogues and shared experiences that cultural preservation could be a unifying force even amidst diversity.

As they navigated the ever-changing landscape, they carried with them the knowledge that their ancestors had persevered through similar trials, leaving a legacy of resilience and determination for future generations to follow. In unfamiliar surroundings, they worked tirelessly to establish new communities and build a future for the generations to come. This indomitable spirit defined the Osage Nation during this tumultuous period.

Language stood as a cornerstone of the Osage identity. The Nation's complex and rich linguistic heritage was deeply intertwined with their culture, oral traditions, and intergenerational knowledge transfer. Realizing the vulnerability of their language in the face of external pressures, the Osage Nation embarked on a concerted effort to document, teach, and revitalize their native tongue. Elders played a pivotal role, serving as invaluable repositories of linguistic wisdom. Aware that history could easily be distorted or lost, the Nation took deliberate steps to chronicle their past. Oral histories were meticulously recorded, offering insights into their migratory journeys, social structures, and interactions with neighboring tribes. The creation of written records, albeit in English due to pragmatic considerations, ensured that their narrative would survive the passage of time.

In the face of external pressures to conform, the Osage displayed remarkable adaptability while fiercely safeguarding their core values. The duality of embracing change while maintaining traditional practices is evident in their art, ceremonies, and daily life. By weaving new elements into their cultural fabric, they managed to preserve their distinctiveness. Recognizing the significance of education, the Osage Nation established schools to pass down their heritage to the younger generation. These institutions served as conduits for transmitting language, stories, and customs. The elders' wisdom was integrated into the curriculum, ensuring the youth were grounded in their cultural roots even as they navigated an ever evolving world. The challenges posed by the Indian Removal Act fostered a sense of unity among the people. Recognizing the strength of solidarity, they organized communal gatherings, cultural events, and tribal councils. These platforms helped make collective decisions and reaffirmed their shared commitment to preserving their way of life.

As the 19th century waned, the U.S. government implemented the Dawes Act to assimilate Native Americans into mainstream American society. The United States government aimed to dismantle the reservation system and integrate Native Americans into mainstream American society. The allotment concept originated in the General Allotment Act, also known as the Dawes Act, of 1887, which sought to break up tribal lands into smaller individual plots. Proponents of allotment believed that private land ownership would encourage assimilation and, in their eyes, "civilize" indigenous communities. The architect of the General Allotment Act, Senator Henry L. Dawes, emerged as a formidable figure in the political arena during the late 19th century. Dawes, representing Massachusetts, harbored ambitions of societal progress and envisioned assimilation as a pathway to achieving his goals. His perspective, rooted in notions of individual land ownership and private property, laid the foundation for the legislation that would bear his name. At its core, the General Allotment Act sought to overhaul indigenous land ownership systems. It aimed to break down collective ownership within indigenous communities and replace it with individual land allotments. This profound shift was envisioned as a means to accelerate assimilation, encourage agricultural practices, and integrate indigenous people into the American economic and social fabric.

Politically, the act held multifaceted significance. For proponents like Dawes, the measure was seen as a pragmatic solution to what was perceived as the "Indian problem." By distributing land to individual indigenous families, it was believed that they would be motivated to adopt Western agricultural practices and abandon their traditional lifestyles. This, in turn, was expected to open up vast tracts of land for non-indigenous settlement and economic development—furthermore, the General Allotment Act aligned with broader policy agendas of the era. The late 19th century was marked by a zeal for expansion and modernization across the United States. The push for westward expansion and the nation's growing industrialization fueled the desire for more land and resources. The act created a landscape conducive to non-indigenous settlement, agricultural production, and resource extraction by converting communal indigenous lands into individual plots.

However, the implications of the General Allotment Act were far-reaching and complex. While proponents envisioned societal assimilation and economic growth, the act often led to the fragmentation of indigenous communities, loss of cultural heritage, and the dispossession of ancestral lands. Amid the challenges posed by the forced removals and the Dawes Act, the Osage took a significant step forward in their quest for self-governance and autonomy by codifying their government structure, adopting a written constitution in 1881 and eventually establishing their own tribal government in 1906, asserting their rights as a sovereign nation within the boundaries of the United States.

The Trail of Tears, oil on canvas 1942. (Robert Lindneux)

CHAPTER SIX
OIL BOOM AND OSAGE ALLOTMENT

Deep within the heart of the American frontier, an extraordinary force of nature lay hidden beneath the surface—the elusive treasure known as oil, colloquially referred to as "black gold." As the 19th century progressed to the 20th, the scientific community pieced together the puzzle of sedimentation, pressure, and organic decay; a tantalizing hypothesis emerged: deep within the Earth, organic matter transmuted over eons into crude oil. This revelation spurred intrepid geologists and prospectors to seek signs of this liquid bounty.

In the late 19th century, this enigma reached the shores of Osage Nation lands, a region blanketed in verdant landscapes and inhabited by a proud indigenous community; beneath this serene exterior lay geological formations that harbored the potential for transformative wealth. The sediments of the Osage hills, deposited over millennia, acted as a geological time capsule, preserving the remnants of ancient plants and animals. In these layers, the key to the oil's location lies hidden. Geologists began to study rock formations, seeking telltale signs that pointed toward oil-rich deposits. As science tools advanced, seismic surveys and drilling technologies allowed them to penetrate the Earth's depths in search of this precious resource. The allure of oil extended far beyond its economic potential, though. The dawn of the industrial era saw the world thirsting for energy to power machines, illuminate cities, and fuel progress. Oil emerged as the elixir that could propel societies forward, an essential ingredient in the engine of modernity.

With their unique geological makeup, Osage Nation lands held secrets that beckoned prospectors and oil companies. This revelation marked the dawn of a transformative era that would come to be known as the "Osage Oil Boom." These pioneers, driven by a blend of scientific curiosity and economic opportunity, ventured into the Osage hills armed with drilling rigs, determination, and a vision of striking it rich. This convergence of science, technology, and ambition marked the genesis of the oil rush that would forever alter the Osage Nation's destiny. The land that had long been cherished by the Osage people for its natural beauty and cultural significance soon bore witness to the derricks, drilling operations, and the birth of oil boomtowns. The landscape transformed, echoing the seismic shifts occurring beneath the Earth's crust.

Public auctions by the Osage tribe took place under the "Million Dollar Elm"
tree in Pawhuska. Eighteen 160-acre allotments were leased for more than
1,000,000 each in the early 1920s. (Jim North)

As the oil wells surged forth with untold riches, a wave of prosperity cascaded upon the Osage Nation, transforming their fortunes almost overnight. The once peaceful prairies now bore witness to the intoxicating dance of black gold, catapulting the Osage into the ranks of the wealthiest in the nation. This newfound affluence not only bestowed material abundance upon them but also beckoned a multitude of external influences that tested the very fabric of their traditional way of life.

Nellie Johnstone #1, discovery well drilled by Cudahy Oil Co. in Bartlesville,
Indian Territory, April 15, 1897. (Oklahoma Historical Society)

Like bees drawn to nectar, oil companies flocked to Osage lands, eager to reap the rewards hidden beneath the earth's surface. The once serene prairies transformed into bustling centers of industry and commerce. Wisely managing their newfound riches, the Nation established a solid financial foundation, securing their future for generations Wisely investing their newfound wealth, the Osage channeled resources into crucial pillars of development, leading to investments in education, healthcare, and infrastructure, elevating the well-being of their community. The Osage's exceptional financial acumen earned them newfound respect and admiration. Recognizing their capacity for self-governance, the government took a historic step, granting them management over their mineral estate. This empowering gesture represented a remarkable recognition of tribal sovereignty, giving the Osage people direct control over their most valuable resources.

Management control over the mineral estate meant more than just economic governance. It signified the Osage Nation's authority to oversee the extraction, utilization, and benefits derived from the resources beneath their ancestral lands. No longer would external entities dictate the terms of exploitation; instead, the Osage were empowered to regulate and manage their resources in alignment with their values and long-term goals. With this newfound authority, they were positioned to navigate the intricate web of economic, environmental, and social considerations that accompanied resource management. The decisions made now bore weight not only in immediate gains but also in the preservation of their cultural heritage, the safeguarding of their land, and the empowerment of future generations. The journey to self-governance was not without challenges. Balancing economic development's imperatives with preserving cultural and environmental integrity required delicate negotiations and visionary leadership.

The granting of management control over its mineral estate also had profound implications for the broader indigenous rights movement. It stood as a testament to the capacity of indigenous communities to assert their sovereignty, negotiate equitable partnerships, and reclaim agency over their resources in a world that had long marginalized their voices. With this newfound power came an added responsibility—the Osage Nation now held the reins of their destiny. The tribe's leaders, infused with a renewed sense of purpose, guided their people with wisdom and vision. Amid the allure of wealth, the Nation remained steadfast in preserving its cultural heritage. They recognized that prosperity need not come at the cost of identity. Instead, they embraced the oil boom as an opportunity to fortify their cultural roots. Keeping their traditions and language alive anchored their identity in a shared past, ensuring their rich history flourished alongside their economic advancements.

But even amidst the glow of prosperity, they remained mindful of the delicate balance they had to maintain. As oil companies clamored for drilling rights, and external interests sought to undermine the Nation's sovereignty and control over their resources. Yet, as in the past, the Osage people rose to the occasion, determined to protect what was rightfully theirs. As the 20th century unfurled its wings, the Osage Oil Boom continued to fuel the fires of prosperity within the Nation. The tribe stood tall, beaming with pride at their remarkable accomplishments. They had managed to strike a delicate balance, embracing the new opportunities that fortune had bestowed upon them while fiercely safeguarding the cherished heritage that defined their identity. Amidst the tempestuous winds of change, the Osage people remained resolute guardians of their cultural identity.

They recognized that amidst the heady allure of wealth and progress, their language, customs, and spiritual traditions were the compass that guided them through the complexities of this transformative era. These enduring threads of heritage were woven into the fabric of their daily lives, serving as a constant reminder of the unbreakable bond with their ancestors and the shared journey of their people. In the subsequent decades, the Osage Nation wisely managed their newfound riches. They invested their wealth in ways that would secure their future for generations to come, recognizing the importance of financial stability and independence. Recognizing that education was a cornerstone for securing the future of their community, they dedicated a significant portion of their oil revenues to enhancing educational opportunities. Modern schools were established, equipped with up-to-date facilities, and staffed with qualified educators. Scholarships were provided to Osage students to pursue higher education, both within and outside their community. These investments empowered the youth with knowledge and skills and reinforced the tribe's commitment to preserving their cultural heritage through education.

With an eye toward improving the overall well-being of their people, the Osage Nation directed resources toward healthcare initiatives and social services. State-of-the-art medical facilities were established to provide comprehensive healthcare services to tribal members. Additionally, programs addressing mental health, substance abuse, and community support were developed to ensure the holistic well-being of the population. Aware of the cyclical nature of resource-dependent economies, the Osage Nation embarked on efforts to diversify their economic portfolio. They invested in businesses beyond the oil sector, including agriculture, tourism, and small-scale manufacturing. These ventures generated additional revenue streams and provided employment opportunities for tribal members, reducing dependency on oil revenues alone.

Investments were channeled into improving infrastructure within the Nation's territories. Roads, utilities, and public amenities were upgraded to enhance the quality of life for tribal members. Community centers, recreational facilities, and cultural spaces were established to foster a sense of unity and pride among the people. Mindful of the environmental impact of resource extraction, the Osage Nation allocated funds for environmental conservation and land stewardship. Efforts were made to restore and protect the natural landscapes that held cultural and spiritual significance. Sustainable practices were promoted to balance economic development with preserving their lands. They invested in legal and advocacy initiatives in light of historical injustices and ongoing challenges indigenous communities face. They engaged in legal battles to secure their rights, including land and mineral rights and advocated for policies that honored their sovereignty and autonomy.

With a deep appreciation for their cultural heritage, the tribe invested in reviving traditional arts, crafts, and cultural practices. Workshops, exhibitions, and mentorship programs were established to pass down ancestral knowledge to younger generations. This investment not only preserved their heritage but also contributed to the vibrant cultural fabric of the tribe. Through prudent investments and a commitment to holistic development, the Nation demonstrated its foresight in ensuring that the benefits of the oil boom extended far beyond immediate gains. Their approach to managing their newfound wealth was characterized by a profound sense of responsibility, sustainability, and a vision for a prosperous and culturally vibrant future. As a result, the legacy of their investments continues to shape their journey in the present day, serving as a testament to their enduring stewardship of prosperity.

As the early 20th century unfolded, the Osage Nation faced a profound and far-reaching transformation—a defining era shaped by landmark legislation, the Osage Allotment Act of 1906. The Osage Allotment Act of 1906 was a direct extension of the principles laid out in the Dawes Act. Under the Osage Allotment Act, the lands of the Osage Nation were to be surveyed and divided into individual parcels of land, referred to as allotments. Each tribal member, regardless of age or gender, was to be granted an allotment of land. The size of the allocations varied depending on certain factors, such as age, marital status, and the number of dependents. The goal was to assign smaller allotments to younger individuals and larger ones to those deemed more capable of managing their lands, often reflecting a paternalistic view of indigenous people's abilities.

While the government presented the policy of allotment as a means to benefit Native Americans by granting them individual ownership of land, the reality was far more complex. The allotment process led to the loss of communal land ownership, disrupting traditional land-use practices and challenging the tribe's collective way of life. Furthermore, the land division had significant implications for mineral rights—the rights to resources beneath the earth's surface. As each individual received an allotment, the mineral rights beneath their land were transferred to the individual allottee, effectively severing the tribe's collective control over these valuable resources.

The concept of private land ownership clashed with the tribe's traditional understanding of land stewardship, where the land was seen as belonging to all, to be held and protected collectively for future generations. Amidst the challenges posed by allotment, the Osage demonstrated incredible resilience. In response to the changing landscape, they established the Osage Tribal Council. The committee's formation was driven by a twofold purpose: first, to address the complex legal and administrative matters arising from federal policies affecting the Osage lands, and second, to establish a forum for the people to have a direct say in decisions affecting their community. This latter goal was particularly significant in light of their unique history and culture. Collaborative efforts and leadership marked the journey to form their Tribal Committee. Community leaders, elders, and individuals who deeply understood the Osages heritage played pivotal roles in orchestrating this development. Their commitment to the collective well-being of the tribe transcended personal interests and fostered a sense of unity that would serve as the bedrock of the committee's functions.

The importance of this Tribal Committee cannot be overstated. It served as a platform through which the Osage people could collectively voice their concerns, participate in decision-making, and advocate for policies aligned with their cultural values and aspirations. This level of direct involvement was critical, particularly in a historical context where indigenous voices were often marginalized in federal policies. Furthermore, the committee was crucial in navigating the intricate legal matters surrounding the Osage lands and resources. As federal policies shifted and external actors sought to exploit Osage lands, the committee emerged as a steadfast guardian of the tribe's sovereignty and rights. Their efforts ensured that their people's interests were safeguarded and that the realities and desires of the Osage community tempered decisions made in distant corridors of power.The Osage Nation Tribal Committee also significantly fostered a sense of continuity and cultural preservation. By championing the Osage's heritage, traditions, and interests, the committee upheld the tribe's unique identity in the face of external pressures for assimilation and change.

"Indian Oil Land Auctioneer Makes Osages World's Richest People," by Roy J. Gibbons. Americus Times-Recorder (Americus, GA), April 1, 1924.

As the newfound wealth attracted a flood of external interests, the allotment process attracted unscrupulous agents and speculators who sought to exploit the situation for their own gain. Some outsiders, driven by insatiable greed, sought to infiltrate the tribe deceitfully. They targeted vulnerable Osage individuals, seeking to marry into the tribe solely for access to oil headrights. Manipulating the allotment process, they acquired allotments known to be rich in oil, further undermining the tribe's sovereignty and economic stability. The Osage were confronted with an unthinkable reality: their kindred became both victims and perpetrators in a vicious cycle of greed and betrayal. These tragic events sent shockwaves through the nation and struck fear into the hearts of the Osage community. Families were torn apart, and the once tight-knit bonds of trust were fractured, leaving scars that would endure for generations.

Yet, even in the face of such darkness, the people refused to be paralyzed by fear. They rallied together, standing as a united front against those who sought to exploit them. Their determination to seek justice for the victims of violence and manipulation became a defining struggle—a battle to reclaim their sovereignty and the safety of their community. Through tireless efforts and the courage to confront these difficult truths, the Osage Nation worked to bring the perpetrators to justice. Their resilience and unwavering spirit led to significant legal reforms, strengthening tribal governance and laying the groundwork for a future where the tribe would be better protected from such external threats.

CHAPTER SEVEN
THE REIGN OF TERROR AND ITS AFTERMATH

As the oil wells gushed forth with prosperity, the tribal members of the Osage Nation enjoyed newfound wealth and a sense of promise for the future. Under the allotment system, individual Osage allottees were granted "headrights"—shares of the mineral rights to their land. Headrights were a system of land distribution used in the early colonial history of the United States. They played a significant role in the acquisition of land, particularly in the context of Native American lands, and have had enduring impacts on land ownership and property rights in the country. Headrights were first introduced in the Virginia Colony in 1618 as a means to encourage settlement and colonization. Under this system, individuals who paid for their own or someone else's passage to the colony were granted a "headright" to a certain amount of land. The idea was to incentivize immigration and promote agricultural development by offering land as a reward for bringing in labor and investment. Headrights were closely intertwined with the expansion of European settlers into Native American territories. As colonists sought to claim the land promised to them through headrights, they often encroached upon and displaced indigenous communities. This expansion led to conflicts over land, resources, and cultural clashes between Native Americans and European settlers for centuries to come.

At the height of the Oil Boom, a reign of terror unfolded—soaking the Osage reservation in blood. As the discovery of black gold beneath their lands had catapulted them into unimaginable wealth, the valuable headrights, granting each tribal member a share of the mineral resources, became a prized possession coveted by those seeking to control the tribe's newfound prosperity. In the shadows, a malevolent cast of characters lurked, driven by insatiable greed and sinister intentions. Among them were individuals who had once been considered part of the community, their malicious intent camouflaged by familiarity. These cunning conspirators plotted and schemed, taking advantage of legal loopholes and the vulnerabilities within the tribe's governance to orchestrate the murders and seize the valuable headrights for themselves.

Among the perpetrators were opportunistic relatives like Ernest Burkhart, cunningly plotting to manipulate family ties for their gain. Others were outsiders who infiltrated the community with deceptive charm. Men like William K. Hale preyed on the people's vulnerability, gaining their trust with false promises of friendship and assistance. Once entangled in their web of deception, these malevolent outsiders manipulated their victims, using any means necessary to gain control over the valuable headrights. This infamous cast of characters went to great lengths to conceal their sinister motives, blending seamlessly into the fabric of Osage society. They attended tribal gatherings, became part of the community, and pretended to be allies.

They plotted in the shadows, fueled by greed, ready to strike at the heart of the tribe's prosperity. These individuals took advantage of legal loopholes and the vulnerabilities within the tribe's governance, seeing the tribe's newfound wealth as nothing but an opportunity to satiate their desires for power and riches, even if it meant causing immeasurable suffering. The Osage people lived in constant trepidation, unsure who among them harbored such malevolence. The feeling of betrayal was palpable, as poison, bullets, and the sinister art of making people vanish without a trace became the tools of terror. Fear and suspicion spread like wildfire, paralyzing the Osage community with uncertainty as each day brought the haunting question of who could be the next victim.

The murders began with eerie regularity—Osage tribal members were mysteriously dying, one after another. At first, the deaths were dismissed as accidents or illnesses, but it soon became apparent that something more sinister was at play. The Osage people lived in fear, not knowing who could be the next victim. As the death toll mounted, a sense of dread and suspicion gripped the community. This unsettling atmosphere revealed the shadows cast by greed and corruption that extended deep into the heart of the Nation. While the precise number of potential deaths remains unclear, it is evident that the extent of the murders far surpasses the names we know.

Among the haunting tales was the case of Mollie Burkharts Family. Mollie and her 3 sisters, Anna Brown, Rita Smith and Minnie were born into the wealthy Osage family of Charles and Lizzie Q. Kyle, whose wealth, like that of all their neighbors, stemmed from the black gold found beneath their land. Their nightmare began on May 21, 1921, after a small luncheon at Mollies' family home. An intoxicated Anna, 36 at the time, had been taken home by Bryan Burkhart, the younger brother of Mollies husband, Ernst Burkhart. Tragedy struck the family a week later on May 27, 1921 when Anna's Body was discovered in a ravine with a bullet hole in the back of her head. The only identifiable things on her heavily decomposing body were the indian blanket on her shoulders and the gold fillings in her teeth. In an act of rampant greed, and corruption the local authorities ruled her death accidental, due to alcohol poisoning. On the same day, the body of her cousin, Charles Whitehorn was discovered by an oil worker on a hill a mile north from downtown Pawhuska. He had been shot execution style, with 2 bullets between his eyes. A mere two months later Mollies mother lost her life to an unexplained ailment.

TWO SEPARATE MURDER CASES ARE UNEARTHED ALMOST AT SAME TIME

Remains of Charles Whitehorn Discovered This Morning On Garnett Oil Lease Adjoining Pawhuska On North; Anna Brown, of Ponca City, Found Dead In Field Between Grayhorse and Fairfax

MURDER CLEARS UP MYSTERY OF DISAPPEARANCE

BULLET WOUND TELLS HOW WOMAN MET HER DEATH

Newspaper Clipping, Pawhuska Journal-Capital (Pawhuska, OK), May 28, 1921

On a cold and ominous day, February 6, 1923, the Osage Nation was plunged into yet another harrowing episode in its tragic history. The lifeless body of Henry Roan, who was also affectionately known as Henry Roan Horse and happened to be another cousin of Mollies, was discovered in his car on the Osage Reservation. His death was a gruesome and chilling affair, marked by a single, fatal gunshot wound to the head, leaving no doubt that malevolent forces were at play. The connection between Henry Roan and the nefarious machinations of a William K. Hale, a prominent cattleman and Ernst Burkharts uncle, further deepened the sinister aura surrounding this murder. Roan had been entangled in a web of financial transactions with Hale, having borrowed a substantial sum of $1,200 from the wealthy cattleman. However, it was not a straightforward financial arrangement that bound them together. Rather, Hale had deviously orchestrated a scheme that sought to exploit Roan's financial vulnerability to the fullest extent. In an act of brazen fraud, William K. Hale contrived to position himself as the sole beneficiary of Henry Roan's life insurance policy, which amounted to a staggering $25,000.

The reign of terror knew no bounds, even beyond the reservation's borders, enveloping the Osage wherever they sought refuge. Those who hoped to escape the horrors by moving to cities found no sanctuary as the sinister web of conspiracy reached far and wide. Rita Smith, and her husband, Bill Smith, were two more victims caught in the web of violence and greed that characterized the Osage Indian Murders. The horrifying events of March 10, 1923, left an indelible mark on the Osage community. On that fateful day, a devastating bomb exploded within the Fairfax residence of Mollie Bukharts last remaining sister, Rita Smith, unleashing a wave of tragedy and death. The explosion claimed the lives of Rita herself and her devoted servant, Nettie Brookshire, while leaving Rita's husband, Bill Smith, with grievous injuries that ultimately proved fatal. Bill Smith's struggle for survival following the explosion lasted a mere four agonizing days before he succumbed to his injuries. In those precious moments before his passing, he bravely and resolutely provided authorities with a statement that would play a pivotal role in the ongoing investigation. Bill's statement not only identified those he suspected were responsible for the horrific act but also shed light on the complex web of conspiracies surrounding these murders. It was later discovered that this explosive device contained a staggering five U.S. gallons (approximately 19 liters) of nitroglycerin.

Photo of destroyed Smith home in Fairfax, OK, The Indianapolis Times (Indianapolis, IN), June 21, 1926.

MYSTERIOUS EXPLOSION

Two Women Killed and Man Serious-ly Injured in Blast Which Wrecks House at Fairfax, Okla.

Fairfax, Okla., March 10.—Two women were killed and a man was seriously injured by a mysterious explosion here today which wrecked the home of William Smith.

Smith was badly burned and his wife and Miss Nellie Brookshire were killed. The cause of the explosion has not been ascertained. Authorities said they were attempting to connect with a possible incendiary motive the fact that Smith's sister-in-law, Anna Brown, was slain here about a year ago.

"Mysterious Explosion," New Britain Herald (New Britain, CT), March 10, 1923.

In 1923, Mollie herself, fell seriously ill and was diagnosed with acute poisoning. Miraculously, she survived the attempt on her life. Ernest Burkhart, her husband, was suspected in the plot to poison Mollie as well several of the other murders. Ernest Burkhart's suspicion of colluding with William K. Hale in the Osage murders was based on a clear set of circumstances and relationships. His marriage gave Ernest a direct financial stake in the Osage oil wealth, making him a potential beneficiary if anything happened to his Osage relatives. To be exact, if Anna, her mother, and two sisters died- in that order- all headrights would pass to him.

"Central Figure in Osage Indian Murder Ring," The Bismarck Tribune
(Bismarck, ND), June 17, 1926.

Suspicion heightened when it was discovered that several Osage individuals, including Ernest's cousin Henry Roan, had taken out life insurance policies listing Hale as the beneficiary. These policies raised concerns, as the deaths of policyholders would result in significant payouts to Hale. Circumstantial evidence added to the suspicions. However, the collusion between some law enforcement officials and the criminals made it nearly impossible for the people to seek justice within the confines of their own territory. Hale had paid off everybody and anyone who shared suspicions and accompanying evidence about what may be going on was met with death threats—or killed, like attorney W.W. Vaughn, who was thrown from a train. The perpetrators of these heinous acts operated with audacious impunity, secure in the belief that their crimes would remain unpunished and between 1921 and 1923 thirteen more murders were reported.

The reign of terror cast its sinister shadow, leaving the community feeling vulnerable and unprotected. Their cries for justice seemed to echo unanswered as the veil of fear and corruption continued to shroud the truth. In the face of the chilling reign of terror that plagued the Osage Nation, the community rallied together to confront the malevolent forces preying upon them. Determined to stand united and protect themselves, the Osage took several measures to band together against those causing the terror. Even with that unity though witnesses were reluctant to come forward due to fear of reprisals. The web of corruption extended far beyond the local level, reaching into the highest echelons of power. Despite these challenges, the determination of the investigators remained unwavering. Advocating for justice and accountability, they refused to be silenced or intimidated, pressing for thorough investigations and fair trials. Despite the corruption that had infiltrated local law enforcement, they recognized the need for a neutral investigative force to uncover the truth and bring the perpetrators to justice.

In the aftermath of the harrowing Osage Indian Murders and the reign of terror that had gripped the Nation, a glimmer of hope emerged with the arrival of the Federal Bureau of Investigation (FBI) on the scene. At the helm of this crucial endeavor was none other than the determined and ambitious J. Edgar Hoover, who sought to transform the fledgling law enforcement agency into a formidable investigative force that would uphold justice and bring criminals to account. The Osage case would become a defining test of the FBI's capabilities, a turning point in the Osage community's pursuit of truth and closure. However, the local law enforcement's involvement in the criminal activities created a chilling atmosphere of distrust among the Osage people, leading many to believe that seeking justice through official channels was futile. In the aftermath of each murder, local law enforcement's response was marred by a disturbing pattern of complacency and obfuscation. Rather than diligently pursuing the truth, some members of the local authorities were complicit in covering up the crimes, dismissing the deaths as accidents or illnesses without thorough investigation. This atmosphere of indifference left the tribe vulnerable and disillusioned as they grappled with the unsettling realization that those sworn to protect them were failing in their duty. Critical evidence was mishandled or deliberately suppressed, impeding any meaningful progress in uncovering the truth. The victims' families were left to grapple with the anguish of unexplained deaths and the knowledge that justice remained elusive. The profound impact of local law enforcement corruption on the investigations cannot be overstated. The Osage people found themselves trapped in a cycle of violence and silence, unable to trust the institutions meant to protect them.

The FBI brought with it a fresh breath of impartiality and professionalism, instilling a newfound hope among the Osage community. In this climate of fear and desperation, the efforts of the FBI and the collaboration with the Osage community would eventually begin to dismantle the network of corruption, uncover the truth, and provide much-needed hope for justice. The FBI agents immersed themselves in the case, leaving no detail overlooked. With unyielding determination, they meticulously examined every piece of evidence, conducted interviews, and collaborated with local law enforcement whenever possible. The pursuit of justice became a relentless quest, and the agents utilized cutting-edge forensic techniques to analyze physical evidence and draw insights from witness testimonies.

At the forefront of the FBI investigation was a young and determined man named J. Edgar Hoover. Appointed as the Director of the Bureau of Investigation in 1924, Hoover was a driving force behind transforming the organization into the Federal Bureau of Investigation that we know today. J. Edgar Hoover was born on January 1, 1895, in Washington, D.C. He joined the Justice Department in 1917, where he quickly rose through the ranks due to his exceptional leadership skills and dedication to the pursuit of justice. In 1924, at just 29 years old, Hoover was appointed as the head of the Bureau of Investigation, which would later become the FBI.

When news of the reign of terror in the Osage Nation reached the nation's capital, Hoover recognized the gravity of the situation and the urgent need for federal intervention. He saw an opportunity to showcase the capabilities of the newly reorganized FBI while bringing justice to a community that heinous crimes had plagued. Hoover took a personal interest in the Osage case, viewing it as a test for the young agency and a chance to prove its worth. He was known for his tenacity and commitment to the pursuit of truth, a characteristic that would serve him well in the complex and multifaceted investigation that lay ahead.

Under Hoover's leadership, the FBI agents investigating the Osage case were given explicit instructions to leave no stone unturned. The scope of the investigation extended far beyond the Osage reservation as they followed leads that led them across state lines and to a web of conspirators involved in the reign of terror. Hoover's determination to deliver justice for the Osage people was unwavering. He ensured that the agents on the case were well-trained and equipped with the latest forensic techniques and investigative tools available at the time. The FBI employed modern methods to analyze physical evidence and used newly developed criminal profiling techniques to understand the motivations and patterns of the perpetrators. These cutting-edge techniques played a crucial role in unraveling the complex web of conspiracy and bringing the perpetrators to justice.

One of the foundational forensic methods utilized by the FBI was fingerprint analysis. By collecting and comparing fingerprints found at crime scenes with those of potential suspects, investigators could establish connections between individuals and specific locations. This method helped to identify individuals who had been present at the scenes of the crimes, linking them to the various murder cases and uncovering their roles in the larger conspiracy. Ballistics analysis played a vital role in connecting firearms to specific crimes as well. Investigators examined bullets, shell casings, and firearms recovered from crime scenes and suspects to determine whether they matched. This analysis not only helped establish links between different murders but also corroborated witness statements and physical evidence.In cases where the cause of death was unclear or disputed, toxicology testing was employed. This method involved analyzing bodily fluids and tissues to identify the presence of substances that could have contributed to the victims' deaths. Toxicology testing played a crucial role in debunking false narratives surrounding the causes of death and shedding light on the true circumstances.

While not a traditional forensic method, witness interviews were a critical component of the investigation. The FBI employed trained agents to interview witnesses, suspects, and individuals who knew the crimes. These interviews were conducted meticulously to extract accurate and reliable information, helping to corroborate evidence and build a comprehensive understanding of the events. The FBI collaborated with experts in various fields, such as forensic pathology and anthropology, to ensure the accuracy and validity of their findings. These collaborations enriched the investigative process, providing specialized insights that contributed to the overall picture of the conspiracy. The use of modern forensic methods during the investigation into the Osage murder cases revolutionized the pursuit of justice.

Moreover, Hoover understood the importance of gaining the trust and cooperation of the Osage community. He emphasized the need for the agents to work closely with tribal members, respecting their cultural practices and building relationships based on mutual respect. The FBI's involvement in the Osage case marked a pivotal moment in the agency's history. It showcased the FBI's potential as a professional and effective investigative force capable of tackling complex, high-profile cases. Hoover's leadership during the investigation earned him admiration and respect within the Bureau and beyond.

Some perpetrators were ultimately brought to justice, providing a measure of closure for the Osage community. However, not all criminals faced punishment, leaving the wounds of the past to linger as a haunting reminder of the dark period in Osage's history. After the dark era of the Osage Indian Murders and the reign of terror, a new chapter began for the Nation, marked by the pursuit of justice, healing, and recovery. The investigations led by the Federal Bureau of Investigation brought some measure of closure and accountability for the crimes committed against the tribe. In the aftermath of the troubles, the Osage people embarked on a journey of resilience and renewal, seeking to rebuild their sense of community, security, and cultural identity.

The investigation and trial of William K. Hale stand as a pivotal moment in the pursuit of justice during the "Osage Reign of Terror." As a central figure implicated in orchestrating the series of murders that targeted the Osage Nation, Hale's case symbolized the determination of both the Osage community and the Federal Bureau of Investigation (FBI) to dismantle corruption, expose the truth, and hold the guilty accountable. William K. Hale, a wealthy and influential white rancher, had exploited the complex allotment system and the mineral rights of the Osage people for personal gain.

The investigation into Hale's involvement was a challenging endeavor. The FBI, however, was undeterred. Agents worked tirelessly to unravel the intricate connections between Hale and the various murders, piecing together a mosaic of evidence that revealed his complicity. Ballistics analysis tied firearms found in Hale's possession to bullets recovered from crime scenes, offering a critical link between him and the murders. Witness testimony, though challenging to secure due to intimidation tactics employed by Hale's associates, began to shed light on his role as a mastermind behind the conspiracy.

The courtroom proceedings, held in 1929, showcased the collective resolve of the Osage Nation to see the Reign of Terror perpetrators held accountable for their crimes. The evidence presented during the trial painted a damning picture of Hale's involvement and his ruthless pursuit of wealth at the expense of innocent lives. Ultimately, the jury found Hale guilty of orchestrating the murders. The verdict sent a powerful message that those who had exploited and terrorized the Osage community would face the consequences of their actions. Hale's conviction provided a measure of closure for the victims' families and a sense of justice to a community that had endured unimaginable suffering.

Law Respects Rich

A United States circuit court has reversed the life sentence on W. K. Hale, millionaire cattleman (above) known as "King of the Osage Country" (Oklahoma), for the murder of Henry Roan, an Osage Indian, two years ago. Hale was said to have been the head of a murder ring formed to kill Osage Indians to procure their lands.

"Law Respects Rich," The Daily Worker (Chicago, IL), April 16, 1928.

HALE AGAIN FOUND GUILTY OF MURDER

"King of Osage Hills," Blamed in Reign of Terror, Gets Life Term.

By the Associated Press.

PAWHUSKA, Okla., January 26.— W. K. Hale, known as the "King of the Osage Hill" and alleged by the Government to have been responsible for a reign of terror among Osage Indians several years ago, again was convicted of murder and sentenced to life imprisonment in Federal Court here late today.

"Hale Again Found Guilty of Murder," The Evening Star (Washington, DC), Jan. 27, 1929.

Another pivotal trial involved Ernest Burkhart, Hale's nephew. Burkhart's connection to his wife, Mollie, gave him access to insider information about the wealth and assets of the Osage victims, which he shared with the perpetrators. He was found to have played a significant role in the murders by assisting in planning the crimes, and even actively participating in some instances.

As the evidence against Burkhart mounted, he was arrested and charged with aiding and abetting the murderers. The following trial was a highly publicized event, drawing attention to the heinous crimes and the more significant issues of racial tension and corruption within the justice system. The trial showcased the challenges of obtaining justice for marginalized communities in an environment where the perpetrators often had social, economic, and political influence. During the trial, witnesses testified about Burkhart's involvement in the conspiracy, his interactions with other conspirators, and his knowledge of the murders. The prosecution presented a compelling case, highlighting how Burkhart's actions directly contributed to the success of the murder plot.

"Confesses Murdering Indians," The Key West Citizen (Key West, FL), June 23, 1926.

On the other hand, the defense attempted to cast doubt on the reliability of the witnesses and the evidence presented. Ultimately, Ernest Burkhart was found guilty of aiding and abetting the murderers. He was sentenced to prison for his role in the crimes that had plagued the Osage community. The trial marked a small victory in the quest for justice. Still, it also underscored the larger issues of systemic racism, exploitation, and the abuse of power that had allowed such a conspiracy to thrive in the first place.

Not all the trials resulted in convictions. Some of the defendants managed to evade justice, either due to a lack of evidence or the complexities of the legal system. For example, Kelsie Morrison who was a close associate of William K. Hale and was believed to have been the one who shot Anna Brown. Morrison was acquitted due to lack of evidence, despite testimonies that suggested his involvement. Local law enforcement officer John Ramsey was also accused of participating in the murders. He was indicted for his role in one of the killings, but the case against him fell apart due to procedural errors and a lack of concrete evidence. Clarence "Bud" Burt, a close associate of William Hale, was also suspected of involvement in the Osage murders. Despite testimonies suggesting his guilt, Burt was acquitted due to a lack of direct evidence linking him to the crimes.

These trials revealed the extent to which the perpetrators of the Osage murders could manipulate the justice system to their advantage. These cases stand as stark reminders of the systemic challenges faced by marginalized communities when seeking accountability for crimes committed against them. The setbacks and frustrations weighed heavily on the Osage community, who had hoped for a swift and comprehensive resolution to the reign of terror. Nevertheless, the trials marked significant milestones in the quest for accountability..

Through the trials, the Osage people demonstrated their resilience and determination to seek justice and ensure that the crimes committed against their community would never be forgotten. The legacy of the trials remains an integral part of their history, a testament to the power of perseverance and the pursuit of truth in the face of adversity. The involvement of the FBI also sparked critical legal reforms. New laws were enacted to better protect indigenous communities from exploitation and violence. These reforms offered more significant safeguards and protections for tribal members, aiming to prevent similar atrocities from occurring in the future. The reign of terror that engulfed the Osage Nation during the early 20th century had far-reaching consequences, not only for the tribe but for the entire nation.

In the aftermath of the reign of terror, one of the significant legal reforms that emerged was the Indian Reorganization Act of 1934, also known as the Wheeler-Howard Act. This landmark legislation aimed to reverse the detrimental effects of previous policies, including the General Allotment Act of 1887, which had contributed to the loss of communal land and resources for many tribes, including the Osage Nation. The Indian Reorganization Act encouraged tribal self-governance and sought to restore tribal lands to their rightful owners. It provided support for tribal governments to create constitutions and develop their own governing structures, empowering tribes to manage their affairs more independently.

Additionally, the act curtailed the practice of allotment, recognizing its damaging impact on tribal sovereignty. Instead, it promoted the retention of tribal lands in collective ownership, helping to preserve traditional land-use practices and protect valuable resources like oil and minerals. Another crucial legal reform was the establishment of the Indian Claims Commission in 1946. This commission was created to address historical injustices and provide a legal avenue for tribes to seek restitution for past wrongs, including the loss of land resources and the perpetration of crimes against indigenous communities. The Indian Claims Commission allowed the Osage Nation and other tribes to present evidence of damages suffered due to unfair and unlawful practices, such as those witnessed during the reign of terror. It was a crucial step towards acknowledging the historical injustices faced by indigenous communities and seeking redress for past grievances.

Furthermore, the investigations and trials during the reign of terror highlighted the need for stronger federal oversight of crimes committed on Native American reservations. The Major Crimes Act, passed in 1885, had already granted federal jurisdiction over specific offenses involving Native Americans. Still, the reign of terror emphasized the necessity of improved law enforcement collaboration between federal agencies and tribal authorities. These legal reforms represented significant strides toward justice and empowerment for the Osage Nation and other tribes.

However, justice was just one aspect of the healing process. The wounds left by the reign of terror ran deep, impacting individuals and the entire community. The healing method requires addressing the trauma and pain, individually and collectively. The Osage community rallied together to support one another through this journey of healing. They held ceremonies, shared stories, and leaned on their cultural heritage as a source of strength and resilience. Their cultural traditions and spiritual practices played a pivotal role in guiding them toward recovery.. The scars left by the reign of terror remained, casting shadows on the Osage community's sense of security. However, the determination to rebuild and move forward prevailed. The Osage drew upon their enduring spirit to navigate the obstacles they encountered along the way.

In the years that followed, the Osage Nation focused on strengthening their tribal governance and preserving their cultural heritage. They continued to advocate for their rights and autonomy, asserting their sovereignty and seeking a more equitable future. They also recognized the importance of solidarity with other indigenous communities. They forged alliances and partnerships, understanding that collective action was vital in advocating for the rights and well-being of all Native Americans. As the 20th century progressed, the Osage Nation underwent significant changes. Economic diversification and strategic investments in education and healthcare contributed to the tribe's growth and prosperity. The tribe took steps to secure their financial future, aiming to create opportunities that would benefit present and future generations.

The Osage embraced their history, both the triumphs and the tragedies, recognizing that their experiences had shaped their path and identity. Their cultural traditions and language remained vital aspects of their heritage, ensuring that their unique identity endured despite the challenges they faced. The pursuit of justice and recovery served as a reminder of their enduring spirit, capacity for healing, and determination to forge a brighter future for themselves and the generations to come.

Chapter Eight
Efforts in Culture, Economy, Government, and Their Future

Deep within the heart of the Osage Nation lies a treasure trove of cultural traditions and a language that echoes the wisdom of countless generations. At the core of Osage's cultural preservation lies a profound sense of pride and reverence for their ancestral traditions. Passed down through generations, these cultural practices serve as a living connection to the past, guiding the Osage people through the present complexities. Ceremonies, sacred songs, and dances are cherished expressions of spirituality and cosmology. The spiritual practices of the Osage Nation are deeply intertwined with their cultural heritage, shaping their worldview, traditions, and way of life. Their spiritual beliefs and practices are essential elements of their identity and continue to play a significant role in their lives today. The land, rivers, animals, and plants are considered sacred entities, and they believe in maintaining a harmonious relationship with them. Many traditional ceremonies and rituals are conducted to honor and seek guidance from these natural forces. The cyclical rhythms of nature are woven into the fabric of Osage's spiritual life, guiding planting and harvesting seasons and other communal activities.

Ancestral veneration is another cornerstone of Osage spirituality. The Osage maintain a strong connection with their forebears, believing their ancestors' spirits continue to influence and protect the living. Ancestral stories passed down through generations contribute to the Osage sense of identity and serve as moral lessons. Ceremonies such as the "Wa-Xo'be" (Ancestor Feast) are held to honor and remember the departed, reinforcing the intergenerational bond. The Osage Nation also has a tribal religion known as the "Wah-Zha-Zhi". This traditional belief system centers on worshiping a Creator, who is considered the source of all life and sustenance. The Wah-Zha-Zhi religion encompasses various rituals, dances, and songs that are integral to the community's spiritual life. Despite the influence of external factors and historical challenges, the Osage people have diligently preserved and revitalized their spiritual practices. Efforts to pass down traditional knowledge, conduct ceremonies, and engage in communal rituals are ongoing, ensuring that the spiritual heritage of the Osage Nation endures.

Through these rituals, tribal members honor their ancestors, seek guidance from the spirit world, and renew their spiritual bond with the land that has nurtured them for centuries. In the face of historical challenges, the tribe tenaciously safeguarded their cultural traditions, preserving their songs and dances through oral transmission. This rich oral history has become the tapestry that weaves together the threads of their collective memory. As the modern world encroached upon the Osage community, efforts to preserve and revitalize their native language, Wah-Zha-Zhe, gained momentum. The language is a testament to the depth of Osage's knowledge, encapsulating nuances of their worldview and cultural expressions. This language, sometimes simply referred to as "Osage," is a testament to the rich linguistic diversity and historical significance of the Osage people.

One of the most distinctive qualities of the language is its complexity and intricacy. Rooted in the Siouan language family, Wah-Zha-Zhe is known for its polysynthetic nature, where entire phrases and ideas are often combined into single words. This linguistic structure enables speakers to convey a wealth of information within a single word, making the language both efficient and expressive. Another unique feature is its extensive system of verb conjugations. The language possesses an intricate array of verb forms that reflect various aspects of time, mood, and subject. This enables speakers to convey actions and nuances of intention, causality, and emotion, contributing to a deep level of communication and understanding within the community. The Wah-Zha-Zhe language is deeply connected to the cultural identity of the Osage people, with its vocabulary encompassing specific terms that reflect their relationship with the land, animals, plants, and natural phenomena. These linguistic nuances mirror the Osage worldview, where nature and spirituality are intertwined. Expressions of gratitude to the Creator, reverence for ancestors, and a deep respect for the environment are embedded within the language.

Language revitalization initiatives became a key priority for the Osage Nation, ensuring the younger generations could embrace their heritage through the gift of speech. Schools, cultural centers, and community gatherings became spaces where the beauty and richness of Wah-Zha-Zhe found renewed vitality. Elders play a vital role in this resurgence, generously sharing their linguistic expertise with the younger members of the tribe. Language immersion programs, storytelling sessions, and language classes have become integral to the Osage cultural landscape, nurturing a sense of identity and belonging among the youth. The Osage people understand that language is more than a means of communication; it is a portal to a world of knowledge and understanding.

As the Osage Nation navigates the complexities of the modern world, they have harnessed their resources and strategic vision to chart a path of economic development and strengthen their tribal governance. Their economic development has been shaped by its wealth of natural resources, particularly the oil reserves that lie beneath its lands. Leveraging its mineral resources, the tribe diversified its economic portfolio, ensuring sustainable growth and resilience against market fluctuations.

While oil remains a significant source of revenue, the Osage Nation has ventured into other industries, including agriculture, tourism, and renewable energy. The Osage Nation has embarked on a range of agricultural industries that intertwine contemporary practices with their cultural legacy and land stewardship. These ventures encompass livestock farming, crop cultivation, and value-added product creation, each holding a dual purpose of economic advancement and cultural preservation. Livestock farming extends to cattle and bison, the latter bearing deep historical and spiritual significance for the Osage people as a symbol of their connection to both the land and their ancestors.

Complementing this, crop cultivation revolves around indigenous plants such as corn, beans, and squash, staples interwoven with their dietary habits and cultural rituals. Community gardens flourish as spaces of local food production and knowledge sharing, fostering self-reliance and intergenerational exchange. The value-added products that bolster economic growth by processing and packaging agricultural outputs are equally vital. The Osage Nation champions sustainable practices that blend modern techniques with traditional wisdom, ensuring ecological equilibrium and a sustainable agricultural future. Moreover, their dedication to agricultural education equips community members with contemporary insights, agribusiness management skills, and the fusion of traditional and modern approaches. Through these multifaceted agricultural endeavors, the Osage Nation navigates a path that honors its heritage, boosts its prosperity, and secures a prosperous tomorrow while staying true to its cultural essence.

The Osage Nation has made significant strides in diversifying its tourism industries, leveraging its rich cultural heritage, historic landmarks, and natural wonders to offer a multi-faceted experience for visitors. These endeavors not only bolster economic growth but also safeguard and share their unique traditions, narratives, and contributions to the broader historical fabric of the United States. Visitors are invited to explore museums, cultural centers, and heritage sites that vividly depict the tribe's history, artistic expressions, and age-old practices. Engaging directly with Osage artisans, storytellers, and educators provides an authentic immersion into the tribe's profound cultural identity.

Their landscape is adorned with historical landmarks that carry deep significance both for the tribe and the country at large. Landmarks like the Osage Agency, the Pawhuska District Court, and the Osage Tribal Museum show the Osage people's resilience, contributions, and experiences spanning generations. The heartbeat of Osage culture is further amplified through festivals and events, where visitors are granted a unique opportunity to partake in traditional ceremonies, dances, and feasts. The In-Lon-Schka, or Buffalo Dance, is a prime example of an event that holds profound meaning for the Osage people and allows visitors to witness and engage in rituals that echo through time.

The Nation's natural beauty opens doors to ecotourism and outdoor activities. With serene landscapes, pristine lakes, and verdant forests, the land becomes a canvas for outdoor enthusiasts, offering hiking, fishing, and camping activities. Additionally, culinary experiences celebrating traditional Osage cuisine beckon travelers to explore the intimate connection between food, culture, and history. Educational programs, art workshops, and heritage trails weave together a comprehensive tapestry that delves into the heart of Osage culture, leaving an indelible imprint on visitors and fostering a profound appreciation for the tribe's enduring legacy.

By tapping into the intrinsic potential of natural resources and embracing cutting-edge technologies, the tribe has not only positioned itself as a vanguard in the transition to clean energy but also as a staunch advocate for a greener, more sustainable future. Wind energy stands as a pivotal focus of the Osage Nation's renewable energy initiatives, capitalizing on their expansive landscapes to host wind turbines. This deliberate move not only bolsters the tribe's environmental stewardship but also generates revenue through power sales, creating a cyclical impact that champions both ecological and economic advantages.

Moreover, the tribe has fully embraced solar energy as a complementary force in their renewable energy endeavors. By adorning tribal buildings, homes, and communal spaces with solar panels, they harness the sun's potent rays to generate electricity, reducing their reliance on fossil fuels and curbing harmful emissions. This strategic shift toward solar energy underlines the tribe's commitment to sustainability and its unwavering dedication to nurturing the environment. Beyond energy generation, the Osage

Nation's sustainable ideology permeates their infrastructure. Energy-efficient structures, state-of-the-art LED lighting, and cutting-edge technologies collectively contribute to diminished energy consumption and lower operational costs, cementing the tribe's resolve to integrate sustainable principles into every facet of their development. Revenue stemming from energy production can be channeled into vital tribal initiatives, encompassing education, healthcare, and various services that elevate the quality of life for tribal members.

This diversification has not only strengthened the tribal economy but also provided employment opportunities and economic stability for tribal members. The tribe's economic ventures extend beyond the reservation boundaries, with businesses and investments contributing to the broader regional and national economy. At the heart of their economic development efforts is a commitment to fostering self-sufficiency and independence. The Nation seeks to reduce reliance on external entities, ensuring that their economic prosperity is controlled and managed by the tribe.

Central to the tribe's success in economic development is their modern tribal governance. The Osage people have built a robust and transparent governance structure, informed by their cultural values and guided by accountability and community engagement principles. Tribal citizens play an active role in their governance, exercising their voting rights to elect tribal leaders and shape the direction of their community. Osage leaders are dedicated to representing the interests of their constituents, championing policies that promote economic growth, social well-being, and cultural preservation. Transparency and inclusivity are cornerstones of modern tribal governance. The Osage Nation ensures that tribal members are well-informed about government decisions and have opportunities to provide input and feedback on crucial matters.

The Osage Nation has recently embraced technology and digital platforms to enhance communication and engagement with tribal citizens. Social media, online town hall meetings, and interactive websites have become vital tools for fostering open dialogue and connecting with the Osage community worldwide. The tribe's commitment to innovation and efficiency is evident in its endeavors to provide essential services and infrastructure. Investments in education, healthcare, and social programs demonstrate a dedication to the well-being of their people and a vision for a brighter future. As the Osage Nation looks ahead, its economic development and modern tribal governance continue to evolve.

The Osage people understand that their wealth goes beyond material possessions—it is intertwined with their cultural heritage and language, deep-rooted traditions, and close connection to the land. As they navigate the complexities of the modern world, the Osage Nation strives to strike a harmonious balance between economic progress and cultural preservation. Elders play a crucial role in this endeavor as repositories of cultural knowledge. Their dedication to passing down traditions, stories, and language to younger generations ensures the continuity of the Osage legacy.

In the 21st century, the Osage Nation faces a new landscape of legal and cultural challenges that test their resilience and adaptability. One of the foremost challenges is the protection of their tribal sovereignty. They face legal battles and political hurdles as they continue to assert their rights and autonomy. In the modern era, conflicts over jurisdiction and the recognition of tribal authority have arisen, requiring vigilant advocacy to safeguard their inherent rights. The tribe's relationship with the federal and state governments remains critical for these challenges. In the legal arena, the Osage Nation has become a formidable voice in asserting its tribal sovereignty. They engage in active dialogue with state and federal governments to ensure their rights are respected and protected.

In addition to these broader challenges, the Osage Nation grapples with addressing their community's social and economic disparities. Disparities in healthcare, education, and economic opportunities necessitate targeted efforts to uplift the well-being of all tribal members, ensuring that no one is left behind. Despite these challenges, the Nation also strives to carve out a brighter future for its people through continued advocacy, cultural preservation initiatives, and community-driven development projects.

The challenges they face in the 21st century are not to be underestimated. However, their dedication to preserving their cultural heritage, advancing their economic prosperity, and ensuring the well-being of their people shines as a beacon of hope and resilience. As they navigate the complexities of the modern world, the Osage draw strength from their ancestors' wisdom and the unyielding spirit that has carried them through the ages. Striving for a harmonious balance between time-honored traditions and forward-thinking innovation, they ensure the vibrancy of their cultural heritage even as they embrace positive transformation. The earnest exertions of the Osage Indian Nation across cultural preservation, economic fortitude, and informed governance stand as an indomitable testament to the potency of communal bonds and collective endeavor. Their narrative is characterized by enduring determination, adaptive resilience, and a beacon of hope for future generations.

CONCLUSION

From their ancient roots to the challenges of the 21st century, the Osage Nation has left an indelible mark on the fabric of time—a legacy defined by cultural brilliance, economic prosperity, and unwavering determination. Throughout the pages of this book, we have traced the footsteps of the Osage through moments of greatness and triumph, as well as times of hardship and injustice.

From the days of roaming the vast prairies to navigating the complexities of the modern world, they have faced each challenge with a commitment to preserving their heritage and forging a path of self-determination. In the face of colonization, forced relocation, and exploitation, the Osage people have emerged with an unyielding spirit. This spirit propels them to pursue justice, cultural preservation, and economic prosperity. The Osages' relationship with the land has been at the heart of their identity. Their profound connection to the earth and its resources has sustained them and become a foundation for their economic growth and development. From the vast bison herds that once roamed their lands to the discovery of oil beneath the surface, the Osage people have skillfully navigated the opportunities presented by their natural resources. But the journey continues, and the challenges of the 21st century demand their unwavering attention. The tribe confronts legal complexities, cultural preservation, environmental concerns, and social disparities with fortitude and resilience.

As we reflect on the Osage Nation's history, we are reminded of the power of storytelling and the importance of recognizing the diverse heritage of indigenous communities worldwide. Their journey serves as a poignant reminder of the strength of embracing one's roots, even amidst a rapidly changing world. So, as we bid farewell to this journey through the annals of Osage history, we do so with a sense of admiration and gratitude for the insights gained. We celebrate the timeless legacy of the Osage people. May the echoes of their story linger in our hearts, urging us to stand with respect and appreciation for humanity's rich and diverse tapestry.

Thanks again for taking the time to read this book!

You should now have a good understanding of Osage Nations: History of Osage Indians beginning to End.

If you enjoyed this book, <u>please take the time to leave me a review on Amazon.</u>

I appreciate your honest feedback, and it really helps me to continue producing high quality books.

References

Hunter, Dr. Andrea A.; Ancestral Osage Geography; Retrieved from https://www.osagenation-nsn.gov/who-we-are/historic-preservation/osage-cultural-history

Burns, Louis F.; Osage; Retrieved from https://www.okhistory.org/publications/enc/entry.php?entry=OS001

Sabo, George III; The Osage Indians (2008) Retrieved from http://archeology.uark.edu/indiansofarkansas/index.html?pageName=The%20Osage%20Indians

Wikipedia; Osage Nation. (2023, August 5). Retrieved from. https://en.wikipedia.org/wiki/Osage_Nation

Unknown Author; The Osage; Retrieved from https://www.nps.gov/fosc/learn/historyculture/osage.htm#:~:text=The%20Osage&text=Before%20the%20arrival%20of%20the,the%20pressure%20of%20European%20civilization.

Kansas Historical Society; Osage (2015) Retrieved from https://www.kshs.org/kansapedia/osage/19289#:~:text=The%20Os

age%20were%20a%20patrilineal,various%20Osage%20bands%20 in%20union.

Unknown Author; Osage – Sociopolitical Organization; Retrieved from https://everyculture.com/North-America/Osage-Sociopolitical-Organization.html

Scatney, Matthew; Osage Nation History, Economy, & Culture: Who Are the Osages? (2023) Retrieved from https://study.com/academy/lesson/osage-nation-history-economy-culture.html

Unknown Author; The Royal Proclamation of 1763 (2012) Retrieved on https://www.ictinc.ca/blog/royal-proclamation-of-1763#:~:text=In%20addition%20to%20the%20recognition,%2C%20as%20their%20Hunting%20Grounds.%E2%80%9D

Stephanopoulos, Athena Theodota; SCOURGE OF THE OSAGE FROM THE HAND THAT HELD THE QUILL: THE ECONOMIC SURVIVAL OF THE OSAGE INDIANS CONCERNING THEIR TRANSFORMATION FROM WARLORDS TO LANDLORDS IN THE NINETEENTH CENTURY (2005) Retrieved from https://soar.wichita.edu/bitstream/handle/10057/1176/t07052.pdf.txt;jsessionid=D3831FAAC2119416FD5C1C1842CCCB76?sequence=3

Wiegers, Robert P.; A Proposal for Indian Slave Trading in the Mississippi Valley and Its Impact on the Osage (1988) Retrieved from https://www.jstor.org/stable/25668755

Baker, Lea Flowers; Marquette-Joliet Expedition (2023) Retrieved from https://encyclopediaofarkansas.net/entries/marquette-joliet-expedition-2208/

Unknown Author; Children of the Middle Waters: The Osage Nation Yesterday & Today, Review (2018) Retrieved from https://graduate.utulsa.edu/children-middle-waters-osage-nation-yesterday-today-review/

Unknown Author; Expedition of Marquette and Joliet, 1673; Retrieved from https://www.wisconsinhistory.org/Records/Article/CS520

Tinker, George E.; The Osage: A historical Sketch (2002) Retrieved from https://ualrexhibits.org/tribalwriters/artifacts/Tinker_Osage-Historical-Sketch.html

Mussulman, Joseph A. & Townsend, Kristopher K.; The Osages; Retrieved from https://lewis-clark.org/native-nations/siouan-peoples/osages/

Kansas Historical Society; Osage – Treaties With the United States (2015) Retrieved from https://www.kshs.org/kansapedia/osage-treaties-with-the-united-states/19293

Key, Joseph Patrick; European Exploration and Settlement, 1541 through 1802 (2023) Retrieved from https://encyclopediaofarkansas.net/entries/european-exploration-and-settlement-1541-through-1802-2916

Gran, David; The Osage Native Americans- Removal, Wealth, Murder (2023) Retrieved from https://www.c-span.org/classroom/document/?7493

Unknown Author; Removal of Tribal Nations to Oklahoma; Retrieved from https://www.okhistory.org/research/airemoval

North, Jim; Exiled to Indian Country: Osage Nation (2020) Retrieved from https://www.cherokeephoenix.org/news/exiled-to-indian-country-osage-nation/article_fa4de8df-7364-5161-8020-b4037ca1bc4e.html

Kidwell, Clara Sue; The Effects of Removal on American Indian Tribes; Retrieved from https://nationalhumanitiescenter.org/tserve/nattrans/ntecoindian/essays/indianremoval.htm

Sloan, Kitty; Indian Removal (2023) Retrieved from https://encyclopediaofarkansas.net/entries/indian-removal-

2595/#:~:text=The%20Osage%2C%20for%20example%2C%20w
ho,even%20greater%20threats%20were%20ahead

Unknown Author; The Trail of Tears; Retrieved from
https://scrcexhibits.omeka.net/exhibits/show/sihistory/poststatehoo
d/cherokee

History.com Editors; Osage tribe cedes Missouri and Arkansas
lands(2020) Retrieved on https://www.history.com/this-day-in-
history/osage-indians-cede-missouri-and-arkansas-lands

Unknown Author; Tribes of Oklahoma: The Osage Nation;
Retrieved from
https://sde.ok.gov/sites/ok.gov.sde/files/documents/files/Tribes_of
_OK_Education%20Guide_Osage_Nation_0.pdf

Wikipedia; Osage Indian Murders (August 2023) Retrieved from
https://en.wikipedia.org/wiki/Osage_Indian_murders

Cabral, Carrie; Mollie Burkhart: Survivor of Her Husband's Osage
Murder Plot (2020) Retrieved from
https://www.shortform.com/blog/mollie-burkhart/

Fresh Air; Largely Forgotten Osage Murders Reveal a Conspiracy
Against Wealthy Native Americans (2018) Retrieved from
https://www.npr.org/2018/04/06/600136534/largely-forgotten-
osage-murders-reveal-a-conspiracy-against-wealthy-native-ameri

Contreras, Cydney; What Really Happened During the Osage Murders in Oklahoma (2023) Retrieved from https://www.oxygen.com/crime-news/everything-to-know-about-the-osage-murders

Grann, David; The Marked Woman (2017) Retrieved from https://www.newyorker.com/books/page-turner/david-grann-the-osage-murders-and-the-birth-of-the-fbi

Mcauliffe Jr., Dennis; Sovereignty Denoed (1997) Retrieved from https://www.washingtonpost.com/archive/opinions/1997/07/20/sovereignty-denied/86fc476e-d7aa-49d6-9350-551ab15b5dd9/

Adams-Heard, Rachel; In Trust: TheOsage Nation's Lost Oil Wealth (2022) Retrieved from https://www.bloomberg.com/news/features/2022-09-06/in-trust-episode-one-the-osage-nation-s-search-for-its-lost-oil-wealth

The Historian; 10 Osage Tribe Facts (2023) Retrieved from https://www.havefunwithhistory.com/osage-tribe-facts/

Kratz, Jessie; Terror on the Osage Reservation (2021) Retrieved from https://prologue.blogs.archives.gov/2021/11/24/terror-on-the-osage-reservation/

DeSilver, Debi; Killers of the Flower Moon: The Osage Murders and the Birth of the FBI (2019) Retrieved from https://www.southwestledger.news/news/killers-flower-moon-osage-murders-and-birth-fbi

Klein, Christopher; The FBI's First Bi Case: The Osage Murders (2018) Retrieved from https://www.history.com/news/the-fbis-first-big-case-the-osage-murders

Staff Writer; Part 2 – Allotment, oil, and headrights (2014) retrieved from https://www.examiner-enterprise.com/story/news/2014/11/24/part-2-allotment-oil-headrights/27372598007/

Kansas Historical Society; Osage – History and Culture From the Early 20th Century to Present (2105) Retrieved from https://www.kshs.org/kansapedia/osage-history-and-culture-from-early-20th-century-to-present/19296

Vineis, Chis; The Forgotten Murders of the Osage Indians (2017) Retrieved from https://archiveoklahoma.com/student-work/research-essays/the-forgotten-murders-of-the-osage-indians/

Dept. of Justice; FBI Report on the Osage Indian Murder Investigation (1953) Retrieved from https://www.famous-trials.com/osage-home/2385-fbi-report-on-the-osage-indian-murder-investigation

Hayman, Jann; RedCorn, Alex; Zacharakis, Jeff; New Horizons in the Osage Nation: Agricultural Education and Leadership

Development (2018) Retrieved from
https://jrre.psu.edu/sites/default/files/2019-06/34-5_0.pdf

Dennison, Jean; Stitchin Osage Governance into the Future;
Retrieved from
https://escholarship.org/content/qt51q25248/qt51q25248_noSplash
_c204a4a69f0be7ed5ab8788e47d5cb1a.pdf

The Osage Nation; Osage Nation Launches "Wahzhazhe Always"
Celebrating Culture and Sovereignty; Retrieved from
https://www.osagenation-nsn.gov/news-events/news/osage-nation-
launches-wahzhazhe-always-celebrating-culture-and-sovereignty

Broad, William J.; The Osage Oil Cover-Up (1980) Retrieved
from https://www.jstor.org/stable/1683792

Zomer, Micah T.; Returning Sovereignty to the Osage Nation: A
Legislative Remedy Allowing the Osage to Determine Their Own
Membership and System of Government(2007) Retrieved from
https://www.jstor.org/stable/20070817

The Osage Nation; Department of Resources; Retrieved from
https://www.osagenation-nsn.gov/services/department-natural-
resources

Made in United States
Troutdale, OR
05/06/2024

19684576R00066